A TRAVELLER'S COMPANION TO THE WEST COUNTRY

also by Michael Jenner

YEMEN REDISCOVERED
BAHRAIN – GULF HERITAGE IN TRANSITION
SYRIA IN VIEW
SCOTLAND THROUGH THE AGES
LONDON HERITAGE
JOURNEYS INTO MEDIEVAL ENGLAND

A Traveller's Companion to the West Country

Michael Jenner

For my mother

PENGUIN BOOKS
Published by Penguin Group
Penguin Books Ltd, 27 Wrights Lane, London W8 5TZ, England
Penguin Books USA Inc., 375 Hudson Street, New York, New York 10014 USA
Penguin Books Australia Ltd, Ringwood, Victoria, Australia
Penguin Books Canada Ltd, 10 Alcorn Avenue, Toronto, Ontario, Canada M4V 3B2
Penguin Books (NZ) Ltd, 182-190 Wairau Road, Auckland 10, New Zealand

Penguin Books Ltd, Registered Offices, Harmondsworth, Middlesex, England

First Published in Great Britain in 1990 by Michael Joseph Ltd

This edition first published by
Claremont Books, an imprint of Godfrey Cave Associates Limited,
42 Bloomsbury Street, London WC1B 3QJ, 1996

Map by Peter McClure

ISBN 1 8547 1826 6

Printed in Italy

Half-title page – Saxon sculpture, south porch, Malmesbury Abbey, Wiltshire.

Title page – Silbury Hill sunset.

Contents page – Stonehenge.

Cleeve Abbey, Somerset

Contents

The manor at Cerne Abbas, Dorset

Acknowledgements

The places featured in this book are generally all open to the public and the research and photography were carried out without much privileged access. However, I would like to thank the following for particular assistance afforded me in the course of preparing this book: Bath Stone Quarry Museum, Corsham; Beer Quarry; Bristol Commercial Rooms; Brunel Engineering Centre Trust, Bristol; Cheddar Caves; Harveys of Bristol Ltd; Kent's Cavern; Littlecote; Newcomen Engine House, Dartmouth; Prehistoric Hill Settlement Museum, Capton; Railway Museum, Swindon; Roman Baths and Museum, Bath; *SS Great Britain*, Bristol; University of Bristol (Goldney Grotto); Wookey Hole Caves Ltd.

One of the great pleasures in travelling in the West Country is the tremendous wealth of ecclesiastical architecture, lovingly cared for by the custodians and congregations of cathedrals, parish churches and chapels alike. There is also a rich array of castles and country houses looked after by the National Trust, English Heritage and many private owners who have done so much to keep the archaeological and architectural treasures of the West Country in such excellent condition. Any student of local history will find much of interest in the many museums of the region; and the archaeological collections at Bath, Devizes, Dorchester, Exeter, Salisbury, Taunton, Torquay and Truro are particularly rewarding. I would also like to thank the West Country Tourist Board for their valued assistance, as well as the staff of the British Library for the endless supply of books. Finally, I would like to express my gratitude to Mr David Whitaker of Boscastle in Cornwall for the hospitality of the Old Ship, a friendly haven in fair weather or foul; and to Elizabeth and John Watson of Bristol for their never-failing welcome and stimulating conversation on all aspects of the West Country.

Land's End, the Atlantic outpost of the West Country.

In Search of the West Country

We all know what England's West Country is, or rather we all possess a set of clear images and associations which sum up its essence. These would include cliffs, coves, Celtic saints, smugglers, megaliths on windswept moorland, lonely farms, snug cottages, secretive hedgerows, lofty church towers and above all the sea, the sea. We can agree on all that and a lot more besides, but when we try to define the geographical territory that makes up the West Country then there is endless scope for argument. To the inhabitants of Cornwall Bristol might appear to be somewhere in the Midlands rather than the West Country; and the modern counties of Avon, Dorset and Wiltshire present us with a broad swathe of land where the West Country merges gradually and imperceptibly into that vague entity, southern England. To be dogmatic about what is and what isn't the West Country is to risk stirring up a fair degree of emotional dissent, since the question of regional identity is deeply embedded in the feelings of any community.

A characteristic Cornish view of the matter was given by S. H. Burton, a native of Padstow, in his fascinating book *The West Country* of 1972. He states unequivocally:

> Not by any stretch of the historical, geographical, or cultural imagination can the big-farm counties of Gloucestershire and Wiltshire be included in an entity called the West Country; nor can the urbanised and industrial complex of Severnside, Bristol and Bath be brought within its bounds.

This view of things might be taken to imply that small-scale rusticity is the key to the heart of the region, and that is without doubt the emotional image that most people have of the West Country today. Yet the fact remains that for much of its recent history the West Country, even in its narrower definition, was urbanised and industrialised in advance of the rest of England. Daniel Defoe described Devon at the beginning of the eighteenth century as

> so full of great towns, and these towns so full of people, and these people so universally employed in trade and manufacture, that not only it cannot be equalled in England, but perhaps not in Europe.

Woollen cloth was, of course, the reason for the picture of prosperity, and not just in Devon but also in Somerset and Wiltshire. Pioneering urbanism was in evidence as early as the thirteenth century with the foundation of the town of New Sarum or Salisbury, a medieval equivalent to Milton Keynes in the twentieth century.

It might also disturb some cherished views of the West Country as a pastoral idyll to learn that the Tamar Valley in the nineteenth century was one of England's worst industrial blackspots. The abandoned engine houses of the tin and copper mines of Cornwall are often viewed as almost romantic objects in the landscape, comparable to the tower-houses of Scotland, but they stand like sentinels over hundreds of miles of subterranean tunnels up to 2000 feet beneath the surface. For the miners, 'going to grass' at the end of an exhausting day meant up to an hour's climb up rickety ladders in total darkness, an exertion which aggravated the pulmonary diseases from which so many died painful and premature deaths.

But to return to the question of frontiers for a moment, this account takes the wider definition of the West Country as its starting point, roughly speaking the land that lies south of the M4 motorway and west of a

A huge ammonite from Portland, Dorset, an area which abounds in ancient fossils.

hazy line extending from Wareham on the Dorset coast. There are even some archaeological pieces of evidence to support this territorial definition of the West Country in the shape of huge, linear earthworks thrown up at the time of the Saxon invasions in the fifth century. The two sections of the Wansdyke in Wiltshire appear to be a defence against invasion from the West Midlands, while the shorter Bokerley Dyke, protecting the soft under-belly of the region south-west of Salisbury, still marks the present county boundary between Hampshire and Dorset. Even so, any attempt to define the actual limits of the West Country remains a hazardous undertaking. Some people might be surprised to see Swindon included in the West Country, but if one remembers that the town was virtually created by the Great Western Railway as the nerve-centre of its network, then its omission would be wrong; for as Frank Booker pointed out in his volume on the G.W.R., the effect of this railway, particularly on Devon and Cornwall, was

> the most potent instrument of social change since the Norman Conquest.

Furthermore, the definition of the West Country is further embroiled by the personal perceptions of individuals. If the lands of the Mediterranean may be understood according to Lawrence Durrell as the area where the olive tree is cultivated, then perhaps the West Country might well be defined by some people in terms of cider and cream teas, which help to create a sense of place.

Stonehenge, although now cordoned off and withdrawn into itself, seems to act as a gateway of sorts to the West Country for those travelling on the A303, announcing a change of mood which already anticipates the megaliths of Cornwall. Yet in the context of prehistory, Stonehenge was never a frontier but a centre of the richly impressive Bronze Age civilisation of Wessex. A further layer of ambiguity is added here by the applying of the name of an erstwhile Saxon kingdom to a period of prehistoric culture. Wessex, painfully extended by Alfred the Great from a tiny foothold in Somerset, was at the outset purely a West Country affair by any definition; but as it grew, so its political centre shifted in removes from Athelney to Shaftesbury, then to Winchester and eventually to London. The Wessex of the West Country thus came to lose itself in the wider entity which it had created, dissolved in its own success. The West Country had been also the scene of a crucial conflict in the nation's history which occurred some 500 years before Alfred's victories against the Danes. On this occasion it was the Anglo-Saxons who were the invaders and the Celts of the west under heroic leaders such as Arthur who forlornly tried to defend the native soil.

Although the name of Wessex is still with us, the geographical territory it once occupied exists only in the minds of such bodies as the National Trust, which maintains the memory of Wessex as one of its administrative regions; and there can hardly be anyone today who would claim to be a native of Wessex. In a sense, the notion of the West Country has come to subsume the realms of both Arthur the Celt and Alfred the West Saxon in a merged spiritual homeland. And so, let each individual retain a personal image of what constitutes the West Country and accept that the frontiers chosen for this account have been drawn to include as much as present conventions reasonably might permit.

The revival of Wessex owes much, perhaps everything, to Thomas Hardy. Indeed, we are now presented with Wessex as the landscape of Thomas Hardy, as if the towns and villages, even the hills themselves, were the products of his abundant imagination. Similarly, the literary landscapes of R.D. Blackmore's 'Lorna Doone Country' on Exmoor, and the Cornwall of Daphne du Maurier and of John Betjeman are receiving the same treatment. But even such great writers do not physically create the landscapes which they so vividly evoke, although they do give them a spiritual and emotional dimension, which reveals an inner essence. A curious side-effect of the power of poetic invention is that those areas without their Hardy, Betjeman or Blackmore to give them life can appear bereft of some essential ingredient, albeit of an insubstantial nature.

By contrast, the approach of this book is the search for more material relics of the past, but the subject is not historical in the sense of events such as the Monmouth Rebellion, the landing of William of Orange or the Civil War which all left their mark on the region to a greater or lesser extent. Nor has there been space to tell the story of such local upheavals as the Bristol Riots of 1831. Instead, the emphasis is on physical aspects of the West Country heritage which bear the imprint of the lives of generations past, the environment created by the toil of human beings from the mists of prehistory until the dawning of the present century.

A mention should be made of geology, however, because the rocks and stones of the West Country contain so many clues to the character of the region. Dorset is

Granite outcrop at Hound Tor on Dartmoor, one of a series strewn across the West Country.

The jagged edge of the Dorset coast provides some of Britain's most impressive limestone cliffs, culminating in the strange arch formation at Durdle Door (above)*. The coastal footpath from Lulworth Cove gives access to this five-mile stretch of spectacular scenery.*

Beer Quarry, source of Exeter Cathedral's limestone, has been worked since Roman times.

particularly rich in fossils, mostly of ammonites, and the County Museum in Dorchester displays a set of dinosaur footprints found at Swanage which are about 130 million years old. The granite of Cornwall and Dartmoor has given these places an amazing visual homogeneity which links the cottages and field walls of the present to the standing stones of the Neolithic and the Celtic crosses of the Dark Ages. At places such as Boscastle and Lulworth there are twisted rock formations which are quite enough to convey to the non-geologist the earth-shattering forces which tortured the surface of the planet so many aeons ago. Then there is the colour of the earth itself. Scratch Wiltshire with a plough and it is chalky-white; scratch Devon and the soil is blood-red, a special hue that signifies home to most Devonians.

But not all of Devon consists of red sandstone. A rare outcrop of a creamy-white limestone in the cliffs near Beer attracted the attention of the Romans, who traced back this seam of excellent building stone to where it surfaces in the hills of the hinterland. Here a quarry was started which remained in production until the 1920s. A visit to the subterranean world of Beer Quarry Caves reveals much about the relationship between the geology of the land and the buildings on its surface. With today's easy transport of all manner of building materials, mostly synthetic at that, the local identity of many places is being gradually obscured, but in the past stone did not travel far, due to the high cost of transport, unless the quarries were situated near the sea, as was the case with Purbeck and Portland. At Beer the quarrying over a period of some 2000 years has left its marks in the scars of countless pick-axes. Experts can distinguish the various phases of the working of the quarry from Roman, Saxon and Norman beginnings. In the sixteenth century even Gothic arches were created when a secret, subterranean chapel for Catholic worship was hewn from the rock.

Stone from Beer was used most notably at Exeter Cathedral, but some found its way to Winchester Cathedral and to several grand medieval buildings in London. You don't need to be a geologist to appreciate the beauty of Exeter Cathedral, but an acquaintance with the source of its stone does heighten one's physical awareness of the structure. Each of the great, old cathedrals of the West Country may be traced back to its parent quarry: Wells to Doulting, Salisbury to Chilmark. It is a special experience to stand by the very spot whence sprang not only the cathedrals, but also the castles, stately homes, manors, churches, cottages and even barns. The golden glow of Ham Hill stone lights up a whole corner of south Somerset and north Dorset in great buildings such as Sherborne Abbey and Montacute as well in entire villages such as Martock. Near Corsham in Wiltshire is the Bath Stone Quarry Museum, one of several sources in the vicinity of this popular building stone. But stone did not always need to be quarried; the village at Avebury in Wiltshire derived much of its building materials from the sarsens of the prehistoric rings.

Cottage building, more than anything else, provides a direct reflection of the local environment. Cornwall is known for its cottages of granite and slate, Devon for its cob and thatch, parts of Devon and Somerset for their red sandstone, and Wiltshire for its Bath stone. This variety gives great individual character to the villages of the West Country, which form the most endearing as well as the most enduring aspect of the region's identity. The scenic villages, especially those of Devon such as Bickleigh and Broadhembury, really live up to their billing, as if they were created expressly to

Effigies in Milton Abbey of Lord Milton, later Earl of Dorchester, and his wife.

(Overleaf) *Lord Milton removed the village of Milton Abbas and rebuilt it near by.*

21

Selworthy Green, Somerset, the most endearing of the planned picturesque villages.

convey the essence of picturesque rusticity; and this mood was indeed created artificially in the eighteenth century by some of the landed gentry on their estates in a series of what we might today call 'designer villages'. One such gentleman was Joseph Damer, later Earl of Dorchester, who removed what was a small market town from the site intended for his private park, and built a neat village of forty look-alike semi-detached cottages, which survive under the name of Milton Abbas. Here the spirit of discipline and regimentation dominates the lay-out of two orderly rows of houses facing one another across the road from behind wide grass verges.

John Nash brought the cult of the Picturesque to the West Country village with his idiosyncratic Blaise Hamlet of 1810 built to house retired estate workers. Here the message was variety and artfulness. Nine cottages, each different in design and sporting an array of 'rustic' features, are scattered about a green in a way meant to suggest the informal nature of a genuine village. But the general effect remains artificial-looking despite its undoubted charm. The dream production of this genre is surely Selworthy Green in Somerset, built in 1828 by the 10th Baronet Holnicote, of the famous Acland family. It succeeds to a greater degree than Blaise Hamlet because it plays fewer architectural tricks, relying instead on the natural drama of its Exmoor hillside. Selworthy Green is the epitome of the Picturesque village; and there are many who would still like to see the whole of England presented in this delightful manner. But Lady Acland was not entirely content, for she added one final touch by providing the 'villagers' of Selworthy Green with scarlet cloaks to add a splash of colour to the scene. Even the inhabitants were to be viewed as no more than figures in a landscape.

The search for the heart of the West Country must inevitably lead to closer acquaintance with the parish churches which still give cohesion to village life. Most of the churches are well cared for, and there is scarcely one which does not have some form of restoration project in hand. A marked exception to the rule is the abandoned church at Knowlton in Dorset, which is set within the earthwork of one of three Neolithic henges known as the Knowlton Circles. But church and chapel are not the only Christian sites in the West Country.

Gwennap Pit, Cornwall, was John Wesley's favourite preaching place in the West Country.

(Overleaf) *This view of Wells Cathedral is virtually unchanged since the Middle Ages.*

Swanage's Town Hall is a reconstruction of the Mercers' Hall in the City of London.

Wesley's favourite preaching place in the course of his frequent visits to Cornwall was at Gwennap where a surface depression caused by mine subsidence formed a convenient amphitheatre. Gwennap Pit was subsequently terraced in its present form through the voluntary efforts of the local miners. It is as essential a part of the West Country heritage as the cathedrals and great churches.

A student of regional history will also find much inspiration in such utilitarian places as the original dock in Bristol where the *SS Great Britain* was built, the faint trace left by the Roman aqueduct outside Dorchester or the medieval underground passages in Exeter which once carried the city's water supply. Such works exert a more fundamental impact on our senses and emotions than many an imposing monument raised by a wealthy individual to his own glory. Equally, it is awesome to reflect on the generations who toiled away at Avebury and Stonehenge with no prospect of an end to their labours.

This book has endeavoured to keep to the mainstream of its subject-matter, with the result that many fascinating quirks and oddities have not found a place in the narrative. Suffice it to mention the case of Swanage which was a port for shipping stone from about sixty local quarries before the railway extinguished the trade in about 1880. George Burt, manager of his uncle's firm Mowlem & Co, took pleasure in salvaging a surprising amount of material from demolished buildings in London, which made good ballast on the return voyage to Swanage. Apart from humble street bollards, Swanage acquired cast-iron columns from Billingsgate Market, an archway from Hyde Park Corner and statuary from the Royal Exchange. The *pièce de resistance* is at the Town Hall of Swanage, which Burt adorned with the re-erected Portland stone façade of the Mercers' Hall in the City of London. Hopelessly sooty and grimy at the time, this magnificent example of Restoration architecture has gradually been cleaned by the sea air of Swanage. Another, more baffling gift to Swanage by George Burt was Durlston Castle of 1890 at Durlston Head. Nearby on the clifftop Burt erected his curious Globe in a setting liberally inscribed with a host of random geographical data to distract and illuminate the holidaymakers; for by this time Swanage had already switched from shipping stone to receiving tourists, an activity which has been taken up along the entire seaboard and now dominates our present perceptions of the West Country.

The enigmatic Globe at Swanage is a minor folly donated to the town by George Burt.

A mysterious face emerges from the natural rock at Kent's Cavern near Torquay.

Sites of Ancient Settlement

Even the most casual of travellers in the West Country cannot fail to note that the land fairly bristles with the monuments of antiquity. Alongside these, the apparent absence of a corresponding number of sites of human settlement might suggest that the prehistoric peoples of the region were totally devoted to ritual at the expense of ordinary housing. Thus Avebury and Stonehenge are often perceived as isolated megalithic systems set in an otherwise deserted terrain, visited perhaps only on special occasions such as the winter or summer solstice, as is the present custom of the 'travellers' who converge on Salisbury Plain in response to a strongly felt seasonal urge. In fact, closer archaeological scrutiny reveals that the great centres of ritual were also the centres of an intensive human activity. Unfortunately, however, the scant occupational relics – often no more than the ghost of a field boundary, a scattering of flints and the indentation of a posthole – give the mind no visual reference, and so the impression lingers on of a mysterious civilisation which erected some of the prehistoric wonders of the world, but without leaving much trace of its dwelling places. The traveller in search of prehistoric housing in the West Country must accordingly be prepared to supplement the paucity of physical evidence on the ground with the substantial published findings of the archaeologists. Naturally, as the great epic of prehistory progresses from the Stone Age to Bronze and Iron Ages, so the remains become more tangible and impressive; but at the very beginning the trace of human settlement is usually no more than a handful of domestic rubbish, from which a surprising amount of information may be squeezed by the quasi-forensic techniques of scientific archaeology.

An obscure cave at Westbury-sub-Mendip in Somerset has provided the earliest hard evidence of human settlement in Britain as a whole, dating back to the dawn of the Old Stone Age or Lower Palaeolithic. Scarcely less ancient, as viewed from our remote standpoint today, are the discoveries made at Kent's Cavern in south Devon now engulfed by the suburbs of Torquay. The mind is hard pressed to comprehend the enormous time-span which this remarkable system of limestone caves represents. Excavations by Pengelly in the last century unearthed more than 100 artefacts, mainly handaxes of primitive manufacture, from a deep layer dated to the Lower Palaeolithic, which – as the textbooks say – takes us back in gigantic leaps through the millennia to as long as 500,000 years ago. At this time it may have been that Kent's Cavern was not actually occupied but at least frequented by ancestors of the human race. Animals, it would appear, were the principal residents, notably the sabre-toothed cat and above all the awesome cave bear. Indeed, the great amounts of skeletal remains of this ferocious beast have led to suggestions that the caves were used by the bears for hibernation and that the hunters of the Lower Palaeolithic took advantage of their annual slumber to massacre them and to claim the subterranean refuge for themselves. A confrontation with a cave bear, asleep or not, in a darkness lit only by the uncertain flame of crude torches held by men armed with feeble weapons of flint and stick must have required the utmost in courage. Even now Kent's Cavern can inspire fear. At one point the skull and jawbone of a Great Cave Bear can be seen embedded in what was once the original floor of the cave and is now the roof of a tunnel. There is an imaginative display of finds from Kent's Cavern at the site itself, but the most interesting items are now in the keeping of the Torquay Museum. These include the vertebrae, tusk fragments, milk teeth and molars of a mammoth; all probably washed into the cave aeons ago. There is also the skull of a young woman of about twenty-five years of age discovered in Kent's Cavern. This dates back about 20,000 years and is the nearest we can come to meeting an actual inhabitant of the West Country during the Old Stone Age, although there is also talk of a 31,000-year-old piece of human jaw, which would be the earliest dated piece of a modern human being in Europe.

Occupation at Kent's Cavern has been detected at other times of the Old Stone Age, albeit with huge intervals when extreme periglacial conditions forced human beings to withdraw over the land bridge which still connected Britain to the Continent. Windmill Hill Cave at nearby Brixham has also yielded large quantities of Palaeolithic implements, but further investigation is required to evaluate the materials. The limestone hills of south Devon contain several other caves with proven or potential remains of the period, making this one of the most favoured areas of Old Stone Age settlement in the country as a whole.

An equally popular habitat was on Mendip which provides fascinating glimpses into the darker recesses of the Old Stone Age. Gough's Cave, one of the spectacular complex at Cheddar, focuses our attention on the period approximately 12,000 years ago at the end of the Ice Age when *Homo sapiens* had already evolved and spread north once more into Britain as the glacial cover receded. It was in 1903 that a human skeleton was discovered here, dated by the radiocarbon method to about 8000 BC, which makes this specimen possibly one of the last of the Old Stone Age hunters. The remains of Cheddar Man, as he is popularly known, are on display in the excellent museum on the site. A cut in the skull above the right eye-socket shows that this 5 ft 4 ½ ins-tall man met a violent end to his life of only twenty-three years, quite a good span by the standards of the day. There is a further ghoulish detail to be noted: the body of Cheddar Man was probably ritually defleshed, for the skeleton bears several tell-tale cut-marks. Recent excavations at Gough's Cave in 1987 turned up a jumble of three adult and two child skeletons of some 12,000 years ago which showed suspicious signs of butchering, a discovery which led inevitably to newspaper headlines of cannibalism at Cheddar. Of greater archaeological interest are the large number of flint implements found in Gough's Cave, which was possibly a local factory drawing its raw materials from Wiltshire, as well as a piece of Baltic amber, probably washed up on the east coast of England and traded across the country.

At another point on Mendip, the Wookey Hole Caves, there is further evidence of the Old Stone Age. The Hyaena Den, just outside the main caves, was explored in 1852 by the geologist Boyd Dawkins. Flint implements of Middle and Upper Palaeolithic man were found among the partly gnawed bones of cave bear, woolly rhinoceros, mammoth and hyaenas. This was additional proof that man had existed at the same time as these prehistoric beasts.

Just as the idea of Palaeolithic life is bound up with images of caves and rock shelters, so that of the Mesolithic peoples who followed has become associated almost exclusively with a hunting and fishing nomadic lifestyle whose sole remains consist of hearths or campfires and middens or piles of domestic rubbish which mark their wanderings, as at the notable Mesolithic site near Dozmary Pool on Bodmin Moor. But it is only with the Neolithic or New Stone Age, from about 4000 BC, that the West Country, along with other parts of Britain, acquires its first domestic structures. Although the rectangular wooden huts of the Early Neolithic have all long rotted away, their overall size and construction has been deduced from their post-holes. At Capton in south Devon one enterprising fruit farmer has had a Neolithic house rebuilt on its original site to illustrate the living conditions of the day. The hut itself is atmospheric enough, but the model family portrayed of a couple with one child conforms much more to present reality than to that of the past when such a hut would have provided shelter for an extended family of as many as twenty-five persons. The nearby hill is a site typically preferred by early Neolithic settlers; relatively easy to clear of trees and shrubs, it offers a dry, sunny slope and a commanding but by no means impregnable base. Similar sites were sought throughout the south-west from Wiltshire and Dorset to Cornwall as bands of Neolithic folk advanced through the country, bringing with them not only superior techniques of animal husbandry but more importantly the knowledge of basic agriculture. Land clearance for farming became the order of the day, and permanent settlements were established, thus beginning a process of deforestation and taming of the landscape that has yet to be halted.

Neolithic sites in the West Country cannot rival such impressive relics as the famous stone village of Skara Brae on Orkney, but it is rewarding to explore some of the known places of the period if only to get the feel of the type of locality in favour. In Dorset, within the Iron Age fortifications of Maiden Castle, may be detected a low embankment which enclosed just one side of a Neolithic village of fifteen acres datable to about 3000 BC. The other sides of the enclosure have been obscured by the ensuing Iron Age ditches and ramparts. At Hambledon Hill, also better known for its Iron Age defences, there was a modest Neolithic settlement which is now represented by little more than a ridge. Both sites belong to a category rather bafflingly called 'causewayed camps' since their roughly circular embankment is broken by a number of 'causeways'. Hembury Hillfort in Devon,

Gough's Cave, home of Cheddar Man c.8000 BC.

which was settled as early as 4000 BC is not only the classic Neolithic occupation site in the region but also one of the most romantic hilltops in the West Country, at its best in the spring when all the scars of prehistory are smothered beneath a wall-to-wall carpet of bluebells.

The 'causewayed camp' about three miles NNW of Stonehenge called Robin Hood Ball consists of an oval space of two and a half acres within two concentric rings of bank and ditch, both traversed by 'causeways' of solid chalk, but this lies on land restricted by the military. There is some considerable doubt as to whether people actually had permanent homes on sites such as this, and it is surmised that a more likely use was for coralling animals during seasonal markets. Robin Hood Ball has also been described as a first 'community centre' in the area which existed long before the mighty Stonehenge monuments. The 'causewayed camp' at Windmill Hill

One of the Neolithic circles at Knowlton, Dorset, now shelters a ruined church.

Hembury Hillfort, Devon, bears traces of both Neolithic and Iron Age occupation. It is one of the most attractive archaeological sites in May under its carpet of bluebells.

near Avebury, which has been dated to 3250 BC, has given its name to the material culture of the period. The enclosure itself, composed of three concentric rings of banks and ditches, provided twenty-one acres of living space. However, the dual action of frost erosion and ploughing has gradually worked away at the contours of the earthworks, reducing them to a mere segment which can best be appreciated from the air rather than on the ground. Discarded antler picks and ox shoulder-blades found in the ditches testify to the painfully laborious manual extraction of the chalk from the Wiltshire Downs. It was the spoil of the ditches which provided an outline of the lifestyle of these people. Their crops were emmer wheat, barley and flax; they kept sheep, goats, pigs and above all cattle, including some wild aurochs. Their diet was supplemented by crab apples and hazelnuts. They were not weavers of cloth, but makers of pots and bowls, and they used axes from as far afield as Wales, Westmorland and Cornwall.

This is perhaps the most fascinating aspect both of Windmill Hill and of Neolithic Britain in general: the axes discovered hundreds of miles from their known geological home posit sophisticated communications and trading links over long distances. Cornish axes figure so prominently in Dorset and Wiltshire that one can easily imagine an embryonic 'Cornish Axe Export Corporation' which sent its goods by sea as far as Dorset, and then by overland routes. Pottery must have formed part of the cargoes, for pots made of a clay native to the Lizard Peninsula have been found at Hembury, Maiden Castle, Windmill Hill and other Neolithic sites to the east. It is probable that Cornwall obtained its supply of flints from the chalk district of Beer on the return leg of these voyages by these earliest of merchant venturers.

Doubtless the most spectacular find of an axe far from its 'factory' was the green jadeite specimen discovered beside the remains of a Neolithic wooden trackway preserved in the peat-bogs of the Somerset Levels. This smoothly tooled item was of a Continental stone, possibly from the Alps. But more surprising still was surely the trackway itself, one of several which have been excavated in recent years. The exact purpose of these wooden trackways needs further study, but they were certainly built at a time when the Somerset Levels were not the efficiently drained and manicured farming landscape of today, but a wild bog, treacherous and impenetrable, teeming with edible wildlife. Peat formation over the millennia has effectively pickled miles of these wooden trackways which appear to have provided access both into the bog and between the sandy islands of scattered communities. Since mechanical digging for peat has reached greater depths than manual extraction, a remarkable communications system has been brought to light. Fortunately, much rescue archaeology has been carried out, but conservation of the trackways is another matter. The most sensible method is often just to bury them again. Thus the famous Sweet Track, recently excavated, now lies hidden from view under the Shapwick Heath Nature Reserve. The Sweet Track, dating back to the fourth millennium BC qualifies as the world's oldest manmade roadway. Analysis of the remains showed that it was built within the space of a single summer and stayed in use for as little as ten years. Another wooden track, the Abbot's Way of about 2500 BC, can be seen in replica behind E. J. Godwin Peat Industries near Westhay. This modern reconstruction follows the exact course of the now-buried original track. It is instructive to walk on it for the timbers are quite slippery when wet. To appreciate the woodcraft achieved with the simplest of stone tools one has to see the pictures on display at the Peat Moors Visitor Centre at Westhay. More exciting is the stretch of the late Neolithic hurdle trackway from Walton Heath which is a major attraction in the Somerset County Museum in Taunton.

In the far west of the region lies the Neolithic site of Carn Brea, a truly majestic hilltop affording the most extensive views of Cornwall and dominating the dour industrial conurbation of Camborne and Redruth. Its modest altitude of 720 feet belies the sense of height and remoteness it actually affords. The main visual landmarks today are a 90-foot obelisk of 1837 vintage and an indifferently restored castle, but the overwhelming interest is that this windswept rocky summit was a principal centre of Neolithic habitation, dating back to 3800 BC. The original occupants almost certainly manufactured and traded axes from the local Cornish greenstone, an entirely appropriate activity for an area which is still the heartland of Cornwall's industry. The remains of the improvised defences formed of immense boulders of up to three tons can still be seen strewn among the undergrowth of bracken and fern. Such a superb site attracted occupation during the Bronze and Iron Ages as well, so that the naturally sculpted granite outcrop which crowns Carn Brea must have been a familiar part of the daily scene for countless generations of prehistoric Cornish folk.

The great cultural transition from Stone to Bronze Age occurred in the early part of the second millennium BC. Opinions now differ as to the role played in this technological revolution by the Beaker People from the European Continent, but the main result of the switch to metalcraft for Cornwall is that the region acquired wide significance as the source of tin, which, added to copper, gave the bronze weapons their superior cutting edge. Bronze Age civilisation also witnessed a tremendous agricultural development and the foundation of many new settlements. Although the lowlands of the West Country have erased almost all trace of this intensive Bronze Age activity, the high moors – largely untouched for over 2000 years – have conserved numerous relics of this flourishing era.

On Bodmin Moor there is a great profusion of round stone huts scattered around the granite peaks of Brown Willy, Rough Tor and Brown Gelly. With the warmer and drier conditions which existed at the time, the moorland between 1000 and 1300 feet provided an ideal environment for farming communities. As recent research has shown, the agricultural exploitation of Dartmoor was particularly intense. It has been suggested that much of Dartmoor was settled around 1300 BC in the manner of a single planned act. If true, this raises fascinating questions about the organisation of Bronze Age society in the west. Elaborate field boundaries of stone, known as 'reaves', are still much in evidence at many locations on the moor. Some were cleverly positioned to give each farmer or group a fair mixture of land throughout the altitude range. It is claimed that Dartmoor has

Reconstruction of the Abbot's Way, one of the prehistoric tracks in the Somerset levels.

The Bronze Age settlement at Grimspound on Dartmoor dates back to a time when the warmer, drier climate favoured extensive occupation of the granite uplands.

*The smooth, manicured appearance of the Somerset Levels today (*left*) belies the fact that this was in Saxon times a tract of nigh impenetrable bogland.*

Europe's largest and best preserved prehistoric farming landscape, of which the best example must be the extensive field system at Rippon Tor.

Subsequent deterioration of the climate caused the abandonment of all these now exposed and barren hillslopes which abound with hut circles, reaves and ritual stones. Of all the settlements there is none more evocative than Grimspound deep in the heart of Dartmoor. The pound itself is almost four acres in size, contained within a massive wall of rough dry masonry, which although largely rebuilt in the last century certainly conveys a realistic impression. There were 16 round huts for occupation and a further 6 or 7 for storage, as well as 3 or 4 cattle pens. The site, which can be conveniently surveyed by climbing a neighbouring hill, was ideally placed for the pastoralists of the Bronze Age with access to good grazing and a reliable water supply for most of the year. Such must have been a typical West Country settlement around the beginning of the first millennium BC. As yet there was little preoccupation with defence: the pound would have been to ward off animal predators and possibly rustlers rather than armed aggressors. Something in excess of 2000 hut rings have been discovered on Dartmoor alone, so that the Bronze Age must have been a period of relative harmony and prosperity, blessed by a sunnier climate than has been experienced since those distant days.

Whether the harmony of the Bronze Age was actual or not, the signs are clear that the Iron Age was less favoured in more than one respect. Along with the wetter, colder climate which caused the final abandonment of the marginal moorland by about 500 BC, new stresses in society became apparent with the rapid spread of elaborate hill-forts. These are usually interpreted as the work of successive tribal groups of Celtic invaders, bellicose people who were as much at war between themselves as with the natives of southern England whose lands they invaded. This picture of a warrior aristocracy spreading the use of iron as well as the arts of war, is coming under scrutiny; it is now thought that diffusion and settlement form a more likely scenario. But there can be no doubt that the mighty and sophisticated hillforts of the period represent a quantum jump in military architecture. The earthworks of Maiden Castle in Dorset, with their intricate barbican and redoutable ramparts, have transformed an ordinary hill into a titanic piece of landscape engineering. Thomas Hardy likened Maiden Castle to 'an enormous many-limbed organism of an antediluvian time . . . lying lifeless, and covered with a thin green cloth, which hides its substance, while revealing its contour'. However, the vigour of the deeply incised ditches is such that the huge, prehistoric beast could, it would seem, still rouse itself and shake off its earthly shackles.

Dorset is really the county *par excellence* of the hillfort. The undulating land often needed only the finishing touches of embankments to perfect its natural defences. Two of the most magnificent in Dorset are perched like twins on neighbouring hills above the valley of the Stour. Hod Hill, the largest in the county, comprises fifty-five acres within its multivallate enclosure. It must have seemed impregnable in terms of sling-shot warfare, yet it was rapidly subdued by the Romans in AD 43. Its counterpart, Hambledon Hill, is a masterpiece of deft contouring, especially on the south side where the ramparts sinuously adhere to the curves and folds of the hillside. The steep slope would have taken the sting out of any assault.

Although grand in themselves the great hillforts follow no grand design or strategy but simply lord it over a small locality, indicating a fragmentation of power. South Cadbury in Somerset might appear to command the entrance to the heart of the West Country but that is really to impose the geography of the twentieth century – its proximity to the A303 – on an interpretation of the past. As one proceeds further west,

The courtyard houses of Chysauster, Cornwall, represent a distinctive regional type.

so the hillforts become reduced in scale, pointing to a society of smaller tribal groupings than in the east of the region. Cornwall's larger hillforts such as Chun Castle and Castle-an-Dinas are relatively small. Cornwall also shows how the headlands of the county's rocky coast could be simply converted for occasional refuge by the building of ramparts and ditches on the landward side to create a cliff castle. There are in excess of twenty Cornish cliff castles, notably Trevelgue Head, Gurnard's Head and Dodman Point.

Iron Age Cornwall also provides some well-conserved settlements of a type peculiar to the region. Chysauster is the best example of some twenty ancient settlements in the county which feature the courtyard house, a distinct product of the Land's End peninsula, Penwith. At Chysauster there are nine of these self-contained dwellings where the individual rooms are all entered through a central courtyard, the whole structure being an irregular oval shape. Here we are able to walk along an actual street and to appreciate the characteristics of this house type, huddled together, yet each turned in on itself for maximum privacy as well as shelter from the elements. This house style did not

(Overleaf) *Maiden Castle, Dorset, is the most magnificent of Iron Age fortifications.*

Carn Euny, one of several underground structures or 'fogous' to be found in Cornwall.

spread beyond Penwith and remained in use unaltered into the third century AD, showing how unaffected was Cornwall by the presence of the Romans in the rest of England. Associated with Chysauster is another speciality of Cornish building of the period known as a 'fogou' from the local word for 'cave'. The fogou is essentially an underground passage with optional side passages, constructed of stone walling and covered over by large slabs. The best examples are Halligye at Trelowarren and at the Iron Age village of Carn Euny near Sancreed where the main fogou is over sixty feet long. The purpose of this and other fogous in Cornwall is still not entirely clear, but current thinking tends to favour the idea of a larder or grain store rather than the more fanciful notion of a subterranean redoubt.

The West Country possesses another distinctive Iron Age settlement type in the lake villages of Meare and Glastonbury in the Somerset Levels. The Glastonbury site is a true 'crannog', a man-made island of timber, brushwood and clay, which was built over the previous settlement of oak-framed houses on piles driven into the bog. It is clear that the rising water level dictated the planning change. There are some interesting remains from the lake village in the Tribunal in Glastonbury, but the site itself is less revealing. The only indication that this was once the home of a flourishing Iron Age community 2000 years ago is a collection of low, grass-covered humps in an unmarked field on the road to Godney. Cattle now graze on the lush farmland which was once more suited to waterfowl than to bovines, for it was flooding that caused final withdrawal from the site around AD 50.

This rapid tour of prehistoric housing must end where it began, namely back in the caves; for archaeologists have discovered that the Great Cave at Wookey Hole was reoccupied by Celtic people of the Iron Age. This must have been a most desirable residence, offering commodious accommodation with good ventilation and a private water supply direct from the River Axe. Cave dwelling continued sporadically into the Middle Ages, and exceptionally into modern times. In the mid-nineteenth century there was a report of a lone surviving resident of a cave in Cheddar Cliffs living like a savage. But now the caverns are the domain of tourists, pot-holers, divers and archaeologists.

The Great Cave at Wookey Hole, Somerset, was occupied by Celtic people in the Iron Age.

Surviving stones at Avebury, Wiltshire, one of the wonders of the prehistoric world.

Monuments of Antiquity

'To take in all the beautys of Abury we must widen our imagination and think with the antients.' The wise comment of the seventeenth-century antiquary William Stukeley may be applied to the relics of prehistory in general and not just to Avebury in Wiltshire. But the imagination has to work in two ways: not only do we have to imagine the missing stones replaced, we also have to imagine away subsequent man-made objects and changes to the landscape, so that the stones may be restored to their original physical context. What makes Avebury, despite the damage inflicted, an ideal place to embark on a voyage of exploration into the prehistoric relics of the West Country is that not only is the site of early date, but it also contains examples of the basic types of monuments to be found, albeit with variations, throughout the region. Avebury's megalithic complex overshadows the wonders of Stonehenge in overall size and conception as well as in antiquity. As John Aubrey, another famous antiquary of the seventeenth-century declared: 'This old Monument (Avebury) does as much exceed in bigness the so renowned Stonehenge, as a Cathedral doeth a parish church . . .'

To get an initial idea of the overall power and complexity of Avebury it is better to arrive on foot rather than to drive, as indeed one can, right into the centre of the henge itself. Ideally, the best approach would be along the Ridgeway, the long-distance path which follows a prehistoric track from the Chilterns. Failing that, one can pull off the A4 by a transport café where the Ridgeway crosses the road and walk a few steps to the site of a monument on Overton Hill known as the Sanctuary. From this vantage point there is a fine view which encompasses the major monuments of the glory that was Avebury.

Immediately to the west lies the low mound of the West Kennet Long Barrow, a classic example of a stone-chambered collective tomb, the largest in England. The 330-foot long barrow poses an immediate problem of interpretation, for the space allocated to actual burials is a mere cluster of five restricted chambers at the east end of the structure, grouped around a small central passage reached through a semicircular forecourt. The burials would have occupied a scant 10 per cent of the overall monument. The rest of the barrow is a solid structure composed of sarsen boulders and chalk rubble covered with soil. It suggests some form of symbolic function. But a symbol of what? Explanations range from the practical 'territorial marker' to the more fanciful idea that the builders of the tomb wished to create a womb-like cavern, perhaps a distant memory of their Palaeolithic habitat; and to achieve that effect they had first to construct an artificial hill in which to set their cavern. Central importance is accorded to the positioning of the West Kennet Long Barrow at a prominent but slightly removed spot where the spirits of the ancestors would be continual reference points for the living, while at the same time enjoying their own communion with the celestial realm above. Indeed, the monument has been carefully placed on a spur of the hill rather than the summit, so that it stands out against the horizon when viewed from the valley.

When the West Kennet Long Barrow was investigated by Stuart Piggot in 1955, remains of at least forty-six individuals were discovered. With the exception of one completely articulated skeleton, all else

The chamber of the West Kennet long barrow forms part of the Avebury group of monuments.

was in partial and disjointed form, indicating that the bones had been re-arranged and removed for ritual purposes. Much damage had been done previously in 1685 by a Dr Toope of Marlborough, who had quarried the barrow for bones which he ground up for use in a potion, 'a noble medicine that relieved many of my distressed neighbours'. More recent analysis of the skeletal remains showed, ironically, that many of these early inhabitants of the Marlborough Downs suffered from arthritis and spina bifida. The West Kennet Long Barrow, dated to about 3250 BC, was the earliest of the Avebury monuments, built most probably by the Neolithic occupants of the settlement on Windmill Hill. Another example of the type is Stoney Littleton Long Cairn, just twenty-three miles away in the county of Avon.

From the vantage point on Overton Hill the gaze now swings a few degrees to the north. Right next to the A4 sits the huge, uncompromising flat-topped cone of Silbury Hill. Even the Romans were forced to seek a new alignment for their road to Bath when confronted with this obdurate mass of prehistoric engineering; for this is no freak product of nature but the largest man-made mound in Europe. Dated to around 2660 BC, it required an estimated 18 million man-hours to shift the 327,000 cubic yards of chalk rubble in about 35 million basketloads, roughly equivalent to the volume of the smallest of the three pyramids at Giza in Egypt. The attempt to explain Silbury Hill as a gigantic burial mound for a local magnate finally came apart when Professor Atkinson drove a tunnel into the heart of the hill in 1967–70 and discovered at its centre not bones, but a core of turf containing organic material. Just image an Egyptian pyramid being found to contain nothing more than a bag of compost or dark earth: that is the reality and the riddle of Silbury Hill.

Quite apart from the man-hours of labour involved, the hill represents a considerable engineering feat which required great knowledge of soil mechanics. The hill is composed of a structural framework of chalk blocks arranged as a honeycomb of cells filled in with rubble and levelled off, so that the hill rose in layers like a wedding cake or a stepped pyramid. The uppermost terrace and the top were left flat. The bare facts outlined here argue a number of things. First, there was a food surplus sufficient to support the enormous labour force. Then there must have been a formidable degree of social organisation and technical skill. Finally, the inspiration behind the project, surely not related to death, was almost certainly linked to the symbolic, life-giving earth deposit at the centre. What better way of invoking the spirits of nature to safeguard the fertility of the soil than to erect such a monument in celebration of the soil itself? The very size of the undertaking, however, had much to do with the self-confidence and self-esteem of the people of Avebury. Archaeologists have demonstrated that the original project for a smaller hill was upgraded in the course of construction to make this truly gigantic monument. These early inhabitants of the Marlborough Downs saw themselves in the very vanguard of human achievement, and they proudly shouted that achievement to the skies. The soil sample imprisoned beneath Silbury Hill over 4500 years ago revealed one other small secret: it was found to contain ants with wings, a sure sign that the great work was begun at the height of summer, a precious but tantalising piece of information.

Due north of Silbury Hill lies the heart of the Avebury complex, the great henge and remains of its stone circle, within which there were once two smaller stone circles, the whole covering an area of about 28½ acres. The outer circle alone comprised some 100 sarsens, dragged to Avebury from the nearby downs and erected in their rough, undressed state. Now only twenty-seven are to be found still standing. The survival rate in the inner rings is even worse, with only seven out of fifty-six still existing. As impressive as the stone rings, which today play host to much of the village of Avebury, is the ditch which, although silted up to about half of its original depth of 50ft, represents the removal with antler picks of about 120,000 cubic yards of chalk, quite enough to build a modest pyramid.

It is readily apparent that the stones of Avebury were never architecture in the sense of Stonehenge's trilithons; instead they stake out a space laden with symbolism and ritual significance. The very idea of the henge may have derived from the vast, circular clearings created by the first Neolithic peoples, spaces which announced their victory as civilised agriculturalists over the dark, primeval forces of the forest. An open space creates its own wider horizons and induces a closer

Silbury Hill, perhaps the greatest enigma of the Avebury ritual landscape, still dominates the scene. Excavations have revealed nothing more than a deposit of fertile earth at the heart of this mighty work of prehistoric engineering.

The double row of stones known as the West Kennet Avenue once formed a processional way which linked Avebury's megalithic circles with other sites of ritual significance in the vicinity. Farming activities have removed most of the stones in the course of time.

communion with the sky, stars and planets. Nowadays we romanticise the forest, seeing in it a refuge from the modern world, but to Neolithic folk, confronted with a hostile tree cover, the forest stood in the way of progress both in farming and in communications, and was probably viewed with a measure of dread on account of the wild and dangerous animals it sheltered. What better way then than a man-made clearing to express man's triumph over nature, and what better material than stone to mark the longing for eternity in a world so ephemeral? Thus Avebury's henge and circles might contain the expression of man's most ancient fears and yearnings, a collective response to the riddle of life as experienced by these early farmers.

The Avebury complex is completed by a parallel row of stones which comes snaking from the henge and then straightens out across the fields to link the circles with the Sanctuary, possibly a circular mortuary house, on Overton Hill. The West Kennet Avenue, as it is known, is well preserved in places; but its counterpart further to the west, Beckhampton Avenue, has disappeared almost entirely. Sadly, the destruction of Avebury has been severe, especially by farmers who broke up and reused the stones but also by misguided clerics who encouraged the view that they were the works of the devil. Fortunately, some were buried rather than destroyed, so that they could later be retrieved and restored to their places, but of the original total of over 600 stones today only 76 remain. Avebury, impressive as it is, can be regarded only as a shadow of its former glory.

The megalithic vocabulary of Avebury – with the exception of Silbury Hill – may be found in varying shapes and sizes all over the West Country. On Mendip there are the Priddy Circles and Barrows of Bronze Age date. Stanton Drew, just thirty miles west of Avebury, shows the same basic syntax of stone circles and avenues, albeit on a much reduced scale. The Hurlers on Bodmin Moor also comprise a combination of circles and a linear 'processional' way, but generally the stone circles of Cornwall are independent structures such as the Merry Maidens, as are some of the Dartmoor examples, namely the circle at Scorhill near Gidleigh and the Grey Wethers. Dartmoor is one of the areas most prolific in prehistoric monuments in Britain as a whole. Although first settled during the Neolithic, its heyday came in the Bronze Age of the second millennium BC, and numerous relics of the period in the virtually indestructable granite moorstone still litter the surface of the moor. Generally, the Dartmoor monuments do not have the imposing stature of Avebury or Stonehenge, and it is usual for travellers to speed by unaware that they are seeing anything more remarkable than a boulder-strewn landscape.

At Merrivale, one of the more accessible sites, it takes a while for the eye to decipher the configuration of the stones and to observe the two double rows or alignments running parallel to each other, the one 590 feet and the other 850 feet long. These are located close to a complex of round barrows, cairns and stone circles, preserved closer to their original state than the monuments of Wiltshire because Dartmoor has been relatively untouched for more than 2000 years. Even so, it would be a brave theorist to read into the landscape a coherent masterplan, for there is every sign that prehistoric notions were constantly subject to revision. The modest scale of the monuments must indicate, however, that areas such as Dartmoor and Bodmin Moor – although expressing the same broad megalithic culture – lacked the resources to create the great works of the Wessex region, and may be provincial rather than metropolitan products.

A class of monument well represented in the south-west and particularly so in Cornwall and the Isles of Scilly are burial mounds in the form of chambered tombs. The associated barrows – where they existed – have now mostly disappeared, leaving behind the naked burial chambers,

The stone alignment at Merrivale forms part of the Bronze Age mysteries of Dartmoor.

weighty stone slabs known variously as 'cromlechs', 'dolmens' or 'quoits'. Notable Cornish specimens are Chun Quoit, Lanyon Quoit, Trethevy Quoit and Zennor Quoit, of which only Chun Quoit is still in its original form, the others having had their capstones removed or replaced.

The series of entrance graves on Scilly, a distinct Scillonian type including Bant's Carn, Innisdigen, Lower Innisdigen and Porth Hellick all located on the main island of St Mary's, have attracted much attention over the years. Recent studies of Scilly, notably that published by Charles Thomas, have examined the burial sites on all the islands within their prehistoric context. It was found that there were no 'major ritual monuments construed as the outcome of public works, inspired by any form of central power and authority', i.e. no stone

The burial chamber known as Ballowal or Carn Gluze Barrow, one of the most fascinating of Cornish prehistoric monuments, was probably in use for as long as 1000 years during Neolithic and Bronze Age times.

Lanyon Quoit, Cornwall (left). The re-erected stones are all that remains of a prehistoric burial chamber which was once covered by a barrow of earth and rubble.

rows, circles, henges or other 'hierarchy-betraying' monuments; and it was concluded that this Scillonian culture was exported from Penwith around 2000 BC and not the reverse as had previously been assumed. Furthermore, the burials were integrated into the living, agricultural landscape and contained 'nutrient rubbish' suggesting an invocation to the spirits of fertility in much the same language as the inner core of Silbury Hill. In this instinctive attempt to ward off the spectre of soil exhaustion on Scilly the death of the individual and the life of the community were bound up together in the same world. Thus the cairn fields, such as that on Shipman Head Down on Bryher, should not be viewed as cemeteries in the modern sense but as an ambivalent blend of spiritual and material concerns, with the living and the dead in mysterious symbiosis.

Such is the wealth of prehistoric civilisation in the West Country that it is all too easy to be overwhelmed by complex chronologies, classifications of cultures, site typologies and theories concerning the movement of peoples. The invaluable but often indigestible results of archaeology can usefully be supplemented by a dose of fancy and common sense. Cairns, for example, had the obvious benefit of clearing the land for planting as well as providing sanctuaries for the dead, so that one may safely assume that practical considerations lay behind many of the plans of the prehistoric population. On the other hand, we need to look beyond the obviously practical consideration of material facts towards a more instinctive and emotional understanding as well. William Stukeley's exhortation that we should think with the ancients is nowhere more essential than when confronting a prehistoric complex such as Stonehenge, about which so much has been written that there is now a secondary industry based on summarising what has previously been published.

What we admire today at Stonehenge is the last phase of the monument's evolution, the mighty ring of sarsen stones with lintels which once completely encircled five free-standing trilithons set in the shape of a horseshoe. This point was reached around 2000 BC, more than 1000 years after the digging of the henge itself, and it was a dramatic development which set Stonehenge apart from all other prehistoric monuments in Europe. It became a real structure, recognisable as a building, as opposed to the concept of Avebury as an arrangement of stones. John Fowles has called Stonehenge 'the most natural building, the most woven with light, sky and space in the world'.

Even though it has no roof and no walls. Stonehenge represents a momentous switch into architecture on a monumental scale. It cannot really be compared with anything that preceded it. In spatial terms it stands midway between the landscape engineering of Avebury, totally open to the sky with the heavens themselves the key to the masterplan, and the enclosed buildings of later millennia such as the Gothic cathedrals which delight in their self-containment. As a structure, however, Stonehenge stands alone.

Along with the idea of a proper structure came the associated concern with construction method and type of finish, the beginnings of masoncraft. In contrast to the undressed stones of Avebury, the huge sarsens of Stonehenge, which were also laboriously dragged across country from the Marlborough Downs, were carefully smoothed with stone mauls. The dimensions of the stones were adapted to counteract the distortions of perspective, the lintels curved to create a continuous smooth sweep of the outer ring; and mortice-and-tenon type joints were carved to ensure that the lintels sat securely on the uprights. Whereas Avebury could have evolved from communal imagination, Stonehenge must have been conceived in the mind of an individual or at least a group, for this is a premeditated design, a piece of technology. It has been argued that

The famous trilithons of Stonehenge continue to defy interpretation of their real purpose.

Stonehenge was really a perverse undertaking, a megalithic application of the basic rules of carpentry, and that is was merely a realisation in stone of what had previously been built in wood. But there is nothing wooden about the appearance of Stonehenge; it is unmistakably a megalithic conception. It would be more appropriate to applaud the builders for their original vision rather than accuse them of looking backwards for inspiration.

What seems abundantly clear is that the people of Stonehenge wrested the cultural leadership from those of Avebury, and that their ascendancy is symbolised by Stonehenge itself. It has even been

(Overleaf) *The Merry Maidens stone circle in Cornwall relates powerfully to the open sky.*

Trethevy Quoit near St Cleer, Cornwall, is a burial chamber of truly monumental scale.

suggested that the natives of Avebury were conscripted as slave labour to transport and prepare the stones. But here we are well into the realm of speculation, and it would be a shame to have to view Stonehenge as our first monument to human exploitation. Whatever the circumstances behind the building of Stonehenge, there did occur at the time a significant shift in burial practices from collective to individual, which might indicate that the communality of human society was already breaking down. Such a trend would support the idea of an élite group taking control of the common destiny and asserting regional authority along with new and impressive forms of cultural expression. Indeed, ambitious undertakings seem to be an essential part of the Stonehenge story, for the transport of the smaller bluestones from the Prescelly Mountains in Wales around 2100 BC must rank as one of the epic achievements of prehistoric Britain.

The claims and refutations concerning the astronomical functions of Avebury and Stonehenge will continue to rage – albeit with more emphasis on the midwinter solstice as the great turning point of the year – but to discuss the megaliths as if they were designed specifically as solar or lunar observatories is surely misplaced. These people, at the dawn of knowledge, were responding to and reflecting, however crudely by today's standards, the natural phenomena of the universe which loomed so large in their lives. It is perverse to build them up as a race of superlative scientists calibrating the minutest movement of the planets and then to debunk them as hopelessly inaccurate primitives. Whether accurate or not, whether intelligible or not to us, the aim of the megalithic monuments would seem at least in part to be an attempt to reach out into the cosmos. However, the very idea of a ritual or symbolical landscape is so far removed from our present utilitarian and exploitative approach to the environment that it is almost impossible for us to imagine the urge of our predecessors to express spiritual content on such a vast scale.

As the Bronze Age passed into the Iron Age in the early centuries of the first millennium in north-west Europe, so there occurred a scaling-down of spiritual expectations which appeared to go hand in hand with rising levels of technology. Gradually the monuments of prehistory lost their meaning in the lives of the people. Yet, the maze on Glastonbury Tor, the Dorset Cursus, the Maumbury Rings in Dorchester, the seventy-plus stone alignments on Dartmoor and the countless ritual stones in Penwith, these and many other relics of the Neolithic and Bronze Age in the West Country survived along with the greater works of Avebury and Stonehenge to remind us that the region once played a full and leading role in a wondrous but forgotten chapter of European prehistory. In some remote spots such as the Isles of Scilly, where the custom of collective burial continued long after it had been abandoned elsewhere, we might imagine the old beliefs lingering on. But even here it could only be a matter of time before aspirations changed and memories faded.

Prehistory confronts us with an extremely remote age. From our present standpoint we can only expect to go part of the way towards a full understanding of the ancient stones and earthworks. It certainly makes sense to approach the remains of prehistory as symbols as well as practical systems of technology, but their precise meaning must always stay hidden, for the minds of the builders are inaccessible to us except through the form of the monuments themselves. But although we cannot in the end hope to solve the mystery of the stones, we can do much by restoring to them their essential dimension of natural mystery.

The Gorgon's Head from the Temple of Sulis in Bath, a cultural mix of Roman and Celtic.

Roman Interlude

The clash of Roman arms came to the West Country in AD 43 with the short but effective campaign of the Second Augustan Legion under the command of Vespasian. According to Suetonius, he fought some thirty battles, overcame two powerful peoples and reduced to subjection more than twenty settlements or *oppida*. One of these peoples was certainly the Durotriges, occupying the territory of modern Dorset, but whose sphere extended into south Somerset and a tiny part of Devon east of the Axe. The great hillforts of Dorset were without doubt among the native settlements brought to heel by the tough commander Vespasian, a future Roman emperor.

Excavations carried out in 1934–7 at Maiden Castle by Sir Mortimer Wheeler provided dramatic archaeological evidence of the historical facts outlined by Suetonius. By the labyrinthine barbican at the east gate of Maiden Castle were discovered a great number of heavy Roman iron ballista bolts, including one still embedded in the spine of its victim. This grisly testimonial to the battle may be seen in the Dorset County Museum in Dorchester. Digging also revealed a quantity of hastily buried corpses, a war cemetery of the Durotrigian dead, as well as evidence of the burning of huts which once stood on the spot. These and other indicators enabled a reconstruction of events to be made. After the Roman artillery had fired an intensive ballista barrage, Vespasian's infantry men advanced, fighting their way through the maze of earthwork passages and no doubt shielding themselves from a hail of slingshots launched from the top of the ramparts. The huts just outside the east gate were then put to the flame, and the main entrance was probably forced under the cover of billowing smoke. Once the Roman troops had stormed inside, there was a fierce and indiscriminate slaughter of the occupants. Soon order was restored and the survivors were allowed to bury their dead in shallow pits; according to native custom the burials were accompanied with food vessels and trinkets for the journey into the afterlife. Thus a fateful day for the Durotriges drew to a close. For the Romans it was just another victory for their superior war-machine, but for the peoples of the West Country it was the end of an era of independence.

Maiden Castle, along with the other hillforts of the region, had been designed for the primitive technology of sling warfare, as evidenced by the unearthing of an arsenal of thousands of smooth pebbles collected from Chesil Beach, which must have seemed to represent an inexhaustible munitions supply. However, both weaponry and defences proved ineffective against the lethal artillery of the Romans. A similar story was enacted at the hillfort of Hod Hill where a concentration of ballista bolts was brought down on one particular hut, probably that of the hapless chieftain. At Hod Hill, after the evacuation of the defeated Durotriges, a Roman fortress was installed in the north-west corner, using two sides of the native stronghold. Although the general outline can best be appreciated by aerial photography, it is nonetheless exciting to walk the still-proud ramparts of both the Roman and the previous Iron Age earthworks. Sadly, access is restricted by cattle fencing.

Another tale of bloodshed preceding a victory by Vespasian came to light at the hillfort of Spetisbury Rings, also in Dorset, when the building of the railway cut through a mass grave. In all, there were some 120 skeletons, many with broken skulls, and one victim with a spearhead still lodged in the cranium. A large quantity of native weaponry had also been buried, suggesting that resistance to the Romans was effectively at an end. It would appear that Vespasian had consolidated his position by about AD 47 when he relinquished his command. By this time a provisional frontier system had been established in Britannia along the military road known as the Fosse Way, running south-west from Lincoln and the Humber to Ilchester and the valley of the Axe.

Beyond the Axe and extending to the tip of Cornwall lay the territory of the Dumnonii. The subjection of the westernmost region of the province of Britannia seems to have taken place as part of a subsequent wave of campaigning. Nothing is recorded of this secondary advance of Roman arms in the West Country, but the remains of a familiar massacre have been discovered at the hillfort of South Cadbury in Somerset and date probably from around AD 61. There are positive signs that South Cadbury was occupied by the Romans for a while along with a number of native strongholds including Hembury in Devon. The Dumnonii must have offered some resistance, for the Romans considered it prudent to build a number of conventional forts extending from Wiveliscombe in Somerset, North Tawton and Okehampton in Devon, as far west as Nanstallon in Cornwall. Excavations at Nanstallon, the only known Roman fort in Cornwall, revealed an enclosure 285 ft by 318 ft. The site is not visually impressive, since the eastern rampart was levelled in the nineteenth-century and the other three are overlaid by field walls. This westernmost military outpost of Imperial Rome in Britain accommodated about 500 men, perhaps a mixed garrison of infantry and cavalry. It was occupied for a very brief spell from around AD 55 to AD 80 at the latest. Coastal fortlets along the Bristol Channel were erected to keep a watchful eye on the warlike Silures over the water in south Wales; and their remains have been discovered at Old Burrow and Martinhoe in Devon and at Sea Mills (Abonae) near Avonmouth.

A legionary fortress at Exeter (Isca Dumnoniorum) had long been suspected but it was not until 1971 that it was actually located. The 38-acre site, rather small for a regular legionary fortress, was found to have been occupied from about AD 55 by the Second Augustan Legion. The most spectacular find was the eastern corner of the legionary baths; located under the foundations of the now demolished church of St Mary Major in the Cathedral Close. The site has now reverted to grass, and there is nothing more to be seen; but it is worth sparing a thought as one contemplates the west front of Exeter Cathedral that beneath one's feet once stood a sumptuously equipped Roman bathing establishment, its interior finished with painted plaster and mouldings and veneers of Purbeck marble. Here the soldiers of the Second Augustan Legion would have relaxed off-duty, bathed, gambled and played various sports; doubtless they also discussed the strange ways of the native Dumnonii as well as the meteoric career of their old commander Vespasian who became Emperor in AD 69.

This military occupation of Exeter did not last long, since the Second Augustan was transferred to Caerleon in south Wales around AD 75. Clearly the Dumnonii were by then reconciled to Roman rule for the legionaries were not replaced. Almost immediately, Exeter was launched on a new and dynamic course of development as capital of the *civitas* of the Dumnonii. Civilian settlement began within the confines of the fort. Around AD 80 a basilica and forum were built, encroaching on the site of the legionary baths. Such civic buildings were the physical results of Julius Agricola's deliberate policy of Romanisation in the conquered territories. Perhaps the Dumnonii were not entirely quiescent for the defences of the fort were retained as the first boundary of the emerging civilian

South Cadbury Castle, one of the Iron Age forts successfully assaulted by the Romans.

settlement. It was not until the end of the second century AD that a new defensive circuit was put up around Exeter. This enclosed an area of almost ninety-three acres, reflecting the urban growth of more than a century. Some 70 per cent of the city wall of Exeter has survived; and although much replacement and repair of the masonry has occurred subsequently, it may still be claimed as an inheritance from the Romans. It stands in parts up to 11½ feet high, especially in Southernhay, and forms a striking feature of today's city. The street plan of central Exeter, notably the intersection of Fore Street, High Street, North and South Street, is unmistakably Roman in origin.

Although the city of Isca Dumnoniorum did well out of the Pax Romana, the surrounding territory appears to have missed out on the new opportunities. The rich villas to be found in most other parts of southern England are quite lacking here. Some twenty villas have been identified around Ilchester, but none close to Exeter. One has to go as far as Holcombe and Seaton in east Devon for examples of the type. Cornwall was even less well endowed with the fruits of Roman civilisation. Only the site at Magor near Camborne may be counted; and this is a crude specimen of a roughly rectangular rural dwelling. In fact, throughout the Roman period the native population of Cornwall continued to live in

The King's Bath occupies the site of the original bath first constructed at Aquae Sulis by the Romans to retain the hot, curative waters of the sacred spring.

The city wall of Exeter (left), although rebuilt in medieval times, still contains much original masonry in the lower courses and rests on the foundations of the Roman defences erected to protect the young settlement of Isca Dumnoniorum.

This huge head of Roman workmanship, discovered at Bath, is said to portray an actor.

traditional settlements such as the characteristic courtyard houses of Carn Euny and Chysauster. It seems probable that the land west of the Tamar was largely ignored by the Romans. There is no firm evidence of Roman interest in the tin deposits of Cornwall until the third and fourth centuries, that is after the Spanish mines had been exhausted. A number of Roman milestones belonging to this later period indicate if not a Roman road as such, then at least a trackway in regular use. The milestones or road markers may be seen at various locations, notably in the churches of St Breaca in Breage, St Merteriana in Tintagel and St Hilary in the village of the same name. There is also one near Gwennap Pit and another in a private garden in Trethevy. The Isles of Scilly were part of the Roman world, as evidenced by the shrine on the uninhabited island of Nornour and a piece of a Roman altar discovered on St Mary's and now exhibited in the Abbey Gardens on Tresco. However, it is safe to assume that the vast majority of the rural Dumnonii were wholly unaffected by the Romans. Certainly, the residents of Exeter benefited from the Pax Romana, and it was probably from Exeter that the lady of the Dumnonii originated, whose death was recorded on a tombstone at Split in Yugoslavia in AD 425.

To encounter the full impact of the Romans in the West Country there can be no better place than Bath (Aquae Sulis) where the rainwater which fell on Mendip some ten thousand years ago comes bubbling back to the surface at the rate of 250,000 gallons a day, heated by the earth's core to a comfortable 46.5° centigrade. The site was revered by the local Celtic people of the Dobunni tribes prior to the arrival of the Romans, who with characteristic efficiency set about 'improving' the sacred spring. Whilst admiring the skill and ingenuity of the Roman plumbers and engineers we might also speculate on the outraged feelings of the locals who witnessed the sudden transformation of their spring, probably set in a sacred grove, into a popular health resort of international repute on a major road, the Fosse Way.

The original spring was cleverly tapped by the Roman hydraulic engineers in an oval pool lined with lead. This was kept free of mud and silt by an ingenious sluice which led into an outfall drain so large that men with shovels were able to work in it unimpeded. Once this reservoir of hot water had been consolidated, the pure product of the spring could be channelled at will through a system of baths which became increasingly complex as the centuries passed and Bath developed into one of the great watering places of the Roman Empire. The sacred spring itself was last excavated as recently as 1979–80, and it has yielded up a veritable treasure hoard of votive offerings, over 12,000 coins and a quantity of trinkets. Of great fascination were a number of curses inscribed on thin sheets of pewter. This was a common way of seeking to square accounts with enemies, known or unknown, and for minor as for major misdemeanours. A typical example reads: 'May he who stole my cloak, whether he be man or woman, boy or girl, freedman or slave, become impotent and die.' Names of suspects could be added at will. Now the sacred spring has been covered over once again by the rectangular King's Bath. Here two of the original windows set in the wall of the bath by the Roman builders may still be seen today across the turquoise and steaming surface of the waters.

Perhaps as a conciliatory gesture to local feeling the old Celtic god of the spring, Sulis, was not suppressed but fused together with the goddess Minerva to provide the culturally and sexually ambivalent dual deity of Minerva-Sulis as patron of the baths and spring. There is a remarkable testimony to this conflation of Celtic and Roman beliefs in the sculptured centrepiece of the temple pediment which has come to be known as the Gorgon's Head. The usual female portrayal of the Gorgon has here been dramatically replaced by the typically Celtic, manly countenance of Sulis. The bold, lentil-shaped eyes, the furrowed brow and above all the serpentine locks of hair and beard not only mimic the snakes of the Medusa but also, in association with the male face, recall images of Neptune rising from the deep. This splendid example of Romano-British artistic

(Overleaf) *The Roman mosaic at Littlecote, Wiltshire, is among the best of its kind.*

inspiration is well displayed along with other fragments of the temple façade in the Roman Baths Museum.

Roman civilisation was generously bestowed on other eastern parts of the West Country. In Dorset the territory of the Durotriges was administered from Dorchester (Durnovaria) and possibly Ilchester (Lindinis) as well. Dorchester's first inhabitants would have included some of the survivors of the massacre at Maiden Castle. They and their descendants became systematically Romanised so that any thought of a return to the windswept heights of the exposed Iron Age earthwork would soon have passed out of mind. The more enterprising of the Durotriges may well have aspired to the comforts of urban living as represented by the spacious townhouse whose remains are on display behind the council offices in Dorchester's Colliton Park.

In contrast to the lack of Roman influence in the countryside of Devon and Cornwall there are striking examples in Avon, Dorset, Somerset and Wiltshire of wealthy Roman villas. Mosaics from the villa at Low Ham in Somerset are on display in the County Museum in Taunton. The Dorset County Museum contains mosaic fragments from a villa at Dewlish as well as a large floor from Dorchester itself. Dorset's most famous Roman mosaic, from the villa at Hinton St Mary, was considered so important that it was transported to the British Museum in London. Quite apart from its artistry the Hinton St Mary pavement is highly significant for the fact that its centrepiece features the earliest known mosaic representation of Christ, identified beyond doubt by the Chi-Rho symbol derived from the first two letters of Christ's name in Greek. But along with the Christian motif there were also pagan references which point to a period of religious confusion. Christianity had been promulgated as the official religion of the Empire since AD 313 following the conversion of Constantine but later in the fourth century there occurred a relapse into pagan practices. This is well attested for by the magnificent, restored Orpheus mosaic at Littlecote in Wiltshire. The building which houses the mosaic has been interpreted as a pagan Orphic chapel and bath serving the villa. The laying of the Orpheus mosaic has been dated to around AD 362 during the brief reign of Julian the Apostate. Further excavation at Littlecote might greatly add to the significance of the site. Another sign of the reversion to pagan cults may be seen at Maiden Castle in the foundation of a cella-type temple erected around AD 380, a last flourish of primitive beliefs before the cleansing wind of Christianity came to claim the West Country. A lesser example is the Romano-British temple at Jordan Hill near Weymouth.

Naturally, the Romans bequeathed the region with many relics of more practical enterprises. The most beautifully preserved *agger* of the Roman road from Badbury Rings to Old Sarum is still a feature of the landscape just south of the Hampshire and Dorset boundary close to the A354, where it strikes out across the fields in a straight line as if drawn by a ruler. By contrast, the course of the aqueduct which once brought water to Dorchester meanders around the contours of the hills; it may be seen as a gentle terrace now grassed over clearly visible from the Iron Age fort at Poundbury on the outskirts of Dorchester. In the same city there is also a unique arrangement of a Roman amphitheatre improvised out of a Neolithic henge known as the Maumbury Rings. At Charterhouse-on-Mendip and set on an exposed hillside there is still the outline of what was surely one of the smallest Roman amphitheatres ever built. It was for the entertainment of the soldiers and managers at the famous lead mines of Mendip, represented by the upcast of the surface workings known locally as 'gruffs'. Mendip lead found its way to the Continent as well as being used within Britannia for pewter manufacture and probably for the lining of the baths at Bath.

As the protective shield of the Pax

A Romano-British temple was discovered within the Iron Age ramparts of Maiden Castle.

Romana was withdrawn at the beginning of the fifth century so the picture was one of gradual decay rather than sudden collapse of Roman structures. It is rare to find much archaeological evidence of this period, beyond the hasty repair of Roman defences; but in Dorset we see a forlorn attempt made by the local people to secure their defences against aggressors from the north with a linear earthwork known as the Bokerley Dyke which was built across the Roman road called the Ackling Dyke at the end of the fourth century, even before the official withdrawal of Roman protection. Such measures proved to be of little avail. By the time the Saxon invaders arrived Rome was already a spent and impotent force, and to the people of the west of Britannia no more than a romantic memory.

The primitive vitality of the Cerne Giant has survived the censure of centuries past.

Twilight of the Celts

Incised into a chalk down near the Dorset Village of Cerne Abbas is one of the most amazing and artistically original monuments of prehistoric Britain. Cut in lines two-foot wide and two-foot deep is the huge, manly figure known as the Cerne Giant, a true giant in the literal sense, measuring 180 foot in height. 'Manful' has been a popular epithet in the past to allude to the rampant virility of the giant who sports an erect phallus of mighty proportions to match his impressive stature. The phallus on its own is almost 30-foot long, and one of the popular traditions attached to it is that copulation within its outline would cure infertility in women. The spring rite of dancing round the Maypole with its overt sexual references continued here until 1635 when Puritanism put a stop to the custom.

Attitudes to the Cerne Giant have varied over the centuries according to the changing wind of morality. A 1764 edition of *The Gentlemen's Magazine* reproduced an accurate portrayal of the genitals in their full glory, but only a decade later the first edition of *Hutchins County History* reproduced the drawing with the offending area censored. In the nineteenth century, as to be expected, the phallus was referred to – if at all – in terms of a symbol rather than the real thing. Quite recently, the *Dorset Magazine* reported the stirrings of a new campaign for the giant's genitals to be allowed to grass over, and also the face as well, so that the figure would then appear to be facing back into the hillside, as if in shame. Given the never-failing undercurrent of moral rectitude, it is indeed a miracle that the Cerne Giant has managed to conserve his private parts intact for so long in so public a place. This is even more surprising given that the chalk ditches need regular scouring to save the figure from obliteration. It has been calculated that sixty-six generations of Dorset folk have maintained it through all the social and moral vicissitudes of the centuries.

What interests us now is less the explicit portrayal, to which we should be fully accustomed, than the antiquity and origins of the Cerne Giant, which have implications for our interpretation of the region's past. Until recently, the Cerne Giant was accepted as a crude local version of Hercules, and was thus dated to the end of the second century AD when the Roman Emperor Commodus (AD 180–192) was encouraging the revival of the cult of the classical giant. What has now emerged from further study of the Cerne Giant is that he is both in style and subject a product of purely Celtic artistic inspiration and datable to the eve of the Roman invasion of Britain in AD 43. When taken as evidence of a native Celtic tradition, the figure reinforces the likelihood that the Pax Romana at least in this part of the West Country was very restricted in its sphere of influence. Ilchester and Dorchester might be heavily Romanised settlements, along with their outliers the sophisticated villas in the countryside, but most rural areas must have continued to nurture the old traditions. Seen in this Celtic light, the Cerne Giant also acquires a sinister overtone, for the embanked area above the figure, known as the Trendle, might well have served as an enclosure for impounding victims prior to those ritual sacrifices reported to have been practised by the Druids.

The strong argument for a Celtic continuum in most of the West Country throughout the Roman period would suggest that the first influx of Christian doctrine in the fourth century AD was restricted to the known areas settled by the Romans such as the towns and villas like the famous example at Hinton St Mary. That Christianity found a first foothold in the towns is confirmed by excavations at the huge cemetery at Poundbury just on the outskirts of Dorchester which have revealed hundreds of Christian burials; and at Exeter a Christian cemetery is the only link between the Roman city and the ensuing Saxon settlement several centuries later. If Christianity was initially a purely urban affair, then it might be imagined that all those remote parts of Dumnonia, which remained outside the urban culture of the Romans, continued to be resolutely pagan. After all, *pagani* first denoted 'countryfolk' before acquiring its later sense of 'heathens'.

However, the situation was in reality less clear-cut, for the historian Tertullian of Carthage referred in AD 208 to 'the places of the Britons unreached by the Romans which had already yielded to Christ'. This might mean that Cornwall, perhaps along with Wales, had already received the Christian message, most probably via the old maritime routes of the western seaboard which linked Scotland, Ireland, Wales, Cornwall and Britanny to south-west France and Spain in a trading nexus reaching back to Neolithic times. That Land's End was in touch with international commerce by reason of the tin trade is attested as early as BC 8 by Diodorus the Sicilian who wrote: 'They that inhabit the British promontory of Belerion (Land's End) by reason of their converse with merchants are more civilised and courteous to strangers than the rest. These are the people that make the tin.'

Since it is accepted that the Christian Gospel was relayed across the Mediterranean by missionaries following in the routes of trade, it is quite possible that it also reached that part of the West Country with known international trading links, even during or at any rate soon after the lifetime of Christ. Against this background, the story of Joseph of Arimathea coming to south-west England gains in historical verisimilitude. According to some versions of the legend Joseph was himself a tin merchant. There are also persisting legends that Christ himself came to Cornwall accompanied by Joseph of Arimathea, an idea which surfaced in William Blake's hymn, 'Jerusalem': 'And did those feet in ancient times walk upon England's mountains green?' There are several candidates for the location of Christ's landfall, notably St Just-in-Roseland; and at St Minver there is a Jesus Well which some interpret in the light of the supposed visit to Cornwall. However, proof positive, either historical or archaeological, is entirely lacking. The Chi-Rho stones to be found in the churches at Phillack and St Just-in-Penwith are mid-fourth century at the earliest. Nevertheless, the notion lingers on that Cornwall was visited, if not by Christ in person, then at least by other bearers of the Gospel around the beginning of the first century AD.

Returning to legend, we are presented with the story of Joseph of Arimathea continuing his voyage by boat after the death of Christ, bearing the chalice containing drops of blood from wounds sustained on the cross and finally arriving around AD 37 in Glastonbury. It is here where a tor rises dramatically from the erstwhile bogs of the Somerset Levels, a place known to have been a focus for some sort of earth magic in Neolithic times, that the Christian tradition in England comes firmly to root with the miracle of the thorn tree and the Chalice Well. The thorn tree is said to have sprung from the place on Wearyall Hill where Joseph planted his staff, and although the 'original' tree was destroyed by a Puritan zealot, some cuttings have been replanted to maintain the legend. One such now provides shade at the Chalice Well, which because of the high iron content of the water leaves a reddish deposit and so has become associated with the agony of Christ as the Blood Spring. Whether or not Joseph of Arimathea founded a Christian community must remain open to doubt, but there is a strong case to be made that Glastonbury was already settled by Celtic monks as early as the fifth century, for there are references to monks from Glastonbury taking the Christian Gospel further west into Devon and Cornwall, the Dumnonia of old.

How far Christianity extended in the West Country by the end of the Pax Romana is thus a matter for endless debate, and likewise the question of Christianity's survival in the post-Roman period from the fifth century onward. With the decline of urban life there would have been a corresponding abandonment of the urban version of Christianity as introduced by the Romans. In Cornwall, if the Gospel had been brought independently through merchants, the picture might have been different. However, the vast majority of the people of Dumnonia must have adhered to paganism for the region was to become the target in the fifth and sixth centuries of one of the most intensive and sustained missionary campaigns. It was led by colourful Celtic characters of Irish, Welsh and Breton origin who have done more than any other group of people to give Cornwall in particular its enduring, separate, Christian and Celtic identity.

The names of the saints alone are almost enough to ensure their undying fame. In contrast to the limited and so often repeated register of Roman or Latin saints in most other parts of England, those in the west have a refreshingly original character. Breaca, Brioc, Endellion, Gonand, Gwithian, Ia, Neot, Non, Petroc, Piran and Wennap are truly evocative of a lost age and of a lost culture. The names contain a magical music of their own; merely to recite them sets off a twinkling of saints' bells (which they often carried) in one's ears. Unlike the English custom of dedicating churches to one of the apostles, the earliest foundations in Cornwall and to a lesser extent in Devon, were named after the saint or missionary who had converted the locality. Thus the church dedications not only commemorate the conversion of the district but also give important clues as to the wanderings of the early saints. As many as 174 of the 212 ancient parishes of Cornwall are dedicated to a Celtic saint, and a further 50 in Devon, despite some instances where the original dedication has been subsequently Latinised, as happened to St Piala, the patroness of Phillack who was supplanted by the lacklustre St Felicitas.

The lives of these Christian pioneers are inextricably bound up with images of the sea, for it was along the old sea routes of north-west Europe and deep into the river valleys that they travelled, keeping alive a Christian tradition in the West Country at a time when the rest of England was being steadily engulfed from the mid-fifth century by the remorseless advance of the pagan Saxons. Legends abound of the miraculous ways many of the saints were transported over the ocean waves. The most common version has them landing in Cornwall from Wales on such an unlikely vessel as a millstone, sometimes described as a trough or a coffin. This is thought to have derived from the portable stone altar which was a standard part of a saint's equipment. A delightful variant on the theme has St Ia arriving in Cornwall on an aptly feminine vessel consisting of a mere leaf. The legend relates that she had been late in joining a group led by Fingar which included Piala, Gothian, Erca and Crowenna, whose dedications are to be found at Phillack, Gwithian, St Erth and Crowan respectively. Ia was lucky to have missed the boat, for although by miracle she arrived on her leaf ahead of the others, she was not present at the ambush sprung by the notorious heathen king Teudar. Although some authorities raise doubts about the Irish origin of Fingar's group of missionaries and settlers, there is archaeological evidence of Irish settlement in Cornwall, Devon and Somerset in the presence of Irish Ogham letters of the fifth century carved on the edge of stones with Latin inscriptions. There is a particular concentration in north-east

One of the many legends attaching to Glastonbury is that of the Chalice Well which owes its red colour to iron deposits in the rock but is believed to symbolise Christ's blood.

Glastonbury Tor (right) *has been a place of magical significance for more than 5000 years. There is a legend that the hill shelters the sleeping Knights of the Round Table.*

Cornwall, the best examples being the two stones to be seen at the church in Lewannick and the famous Arthurian stone at Slaughterbridge, as well as one at St Endellion.

For at least two centuries and perhaps longer Celtic saints journeyed to and fro across Cornwall as part of wider peregrinations between Ireland, Wales and Brittany. A major overland route from Padstow to Fowey as an alternative to the dangerous sea passage around Land's End is still commemorated as a long-distance footpath known as the Saint's Way. Of the numerous saintly persons, St Petroc and St Piran have a special place reserved for them in the hearts of Cornish people. Petroc was the patron of Padstow (Petrocstow) where he first settled before moving on to Bodmin for greater isolation on the fringe of the moor; and it was at Bodmin that the centre of his cult was later established. Although his bones were taken off to Brittany by a relic-hunter in 1177 and later returned, they were destroyed along with his tomb during the Reformation. However, the reliquary which once contained his head is still in the possession of the church of St Petroc in Bodmin. This is an ivory casket of twelfth-century date bearing workmanship which has been suggested as of Sicilian inspiration. An exotic reliquary would be quite appropriate for St Petroc, a Welshman by birth, for he travelled twice to Rome in a globetrotting career which also took him to Jerusalem and then on to India and the Far East where he fell asleep on the shore from sheer fatigue. Then in a miraculous voyage in a boat with no oars or steering he was transported to an island where he spent seven years in the company of some holy men, eventually returning to the West Country where he subdued monsters and dragons. St Petroc, although popular in Cornwall, has even more dedications (at least twenty-one) to his credit in Devon.

St Piran, according to popular tradition, came over from Ireland to Cornwall (on a millstone of course) at the ripe old age of 200, and went on to live for another 100. He is the best loved of the Cornish saints, patron of the tinners as well as of three parishes. The Cornish flag features St Piran's Cross, a white cross on a black background, an obvious symbol of the triumph of good over evil, but this has also been interpreted as tin lode standing out against a dark rock. With St Piran archaeology at last has something physical to grapple with. The remains of his oratory have been excavated at Perranzabuloe where it was abandoned to the encroaching sand dunes around the time of the Norman Conquest. A second church, a quarter of a mile to the east, of early twelfth-century date, served as a replacement until 1804 when it was abandoned in its turn. Soon thereafter the present church was built, using some material from the old, three miles inland at Lamborn. Clearly, the church fathers were taking no further chances. The original St Piran's Oratory has in recent years been consigned once more to its sandy grave. The dunes at Gwithian also conceal a foundation of similar early date.

Otherwise, all the sites of Celtic churches have been built over from Norman times on. The famous fourteenth-century chapel on the rock dedicated to St Michael at Roche stands on what is thought to be a much earlier hermit's cell. Likewise the well-houses which cover some of the better-known holy wells such as Dupath and St Cleer are medieval productions. At Madron, however, the lower, pre-Norman courses of a small chapel have survived. The holy well itself is near by, overhung with trees and hemmed in by bushes. Visitors to the shrine have attached numerous strips of rag to the branches as votive offerings to invoke the curative and prophetic powers of the spring. Dedicated to St Madem, the holy well at Madron is but one of 192 in Cornwall; its existence continues the lengthy tradition of religious beliefs that extend far beyond Christianity into the most distant eras of the past.

Dupath Well, Cornwall, is an ancient holy spring marked by a medieval stone shrine.

Most of the famous early Christian crosses in the West Country date to the later part of the Dark Ages rather than the formative years of the new religion. They belong artistically to what is usually termed the Hiberno-Saxon school. Some of the finest examples are to be found in Cornwall, such as the two tall crosses at Sancreed and another at St Buryan without its shaft, all featuring the characteristic round cross head of Celtic design. The shafts of the Sancreed crosses are beautifully incised with geometric patterns and carvings. Generally acknowledged as the finest of all the Dark Age crosses in Cornwall is the lofty Cardinham Cross, a tapering shaft decorated with various designs of interlace, spirals and ring-chain leading to an impressively carved circular head.

The great age of the saints in Cornwall

The St Buryan Cross is a fine example of an early Christian cross of the round-headed type which is well represented in Cornwall. The characteristic long shaft is missing.

The chapel perched on the rock at Roche is a medieval structure but it marks the site of a cell which was probably occupied by a hermit in the very early days of Christianity in Cornwall. The extensive views from the top now survey waste tips of China clay workings.

showed that the Dark Ages in the far west of England were not at all deprived of light; indeed there is a popular saying that there are more saints in Cornwall than in heaven itself. However, the passage of these many holy men has left little for the archaeological record. The settlements of the missionaries would have been simple in the extreme, perhaps no more than a hermit's cell or a hut for the solitary brethren, but there must have been some small communities in monastic settlements along the lines of those discovered in Ireland and south-west Scotland. The much-cited Celtic monastery at Tintagel, which had been generally accepted since its excavation in 1933–4 as Cornwall's unique example of the type, has since the 1970s been refuted as such, with at least an equal weight of expert opinion. Now the secular nature of the Dark Age remains at Tintagel is supported with as much conviction as once attached to their religious character. What has emerged in recent studies is the extreme importance of this rocky headland as reflected in its wealth of sophisticated Mediterranean pottery. Sherds from more than 250 vessels, mainly amphorae for wine and olive oil, have been identified as originating from a gamut of Mediterranean sources reaching from Antioch and the north Aegean in the east to Carthage in the west. Most of the material was dated to the period AD 450–650, but there was also a substantial amount from the late fourth century, indicating occupation of the site even before the end of the Roman period. In all a far greater quantity of these superior imported wares has been unearthed at Tintagel than at any other site in the British Isles. The conclusion is inevitably that, if not a monastic settlement, then Tintagel must surely have been the stronghold of a succession of powerful chieftains, indeed of kings. And so archaeology reluctantly gives substance to the shadowy figure of a king such as Arthur, for it is here at Tintagel that the legend-makers located not just his royal seat but also the place of his birth.

The evidence, or lack of it, for the existence in fact of Arthur has been carefully sifted many times in recent years, and the findings are usually slanted to support the particular viewpoint of the writer. Those opposed to the veracity of the Arthurian story point to the tenuous and unreliable references which suggest that at the most Arthur was only a war-leader or *dux bellorum* rather than a king. The sceptics also underline the extravagant imagination of the original myth-maker in the twelfth century, Geoffrey of Monmouth, whose account *History of the Kings of Britain* set the whole Arthurian industry in motion, with later embellishments coming notably from Malory and Tennyson. Over the years some 150 places from Scotland to the Scillies have acquired an Arthurian association, but the greatest concentration and with it the heartland of the Arthurian story is firmly established in the West Country.

It must be said that the historical scenario of a king or kings defending the cause of Christianity in the context of a post-Roman culture in a Celtic land is unmistakably accurate. The battle of Badon in the early sixth century which halted the westward advance of the heathen Saxons, at least temporarily, is also real enough; even if the exact site of the battle cannot be located. In this bloody battle, according to the *History of the Britons* by Nennius, 'Arthur carried the cross of Our Lord Jesus Christ on his shoulders for three days and three nights and the Britons were victorious.'

Popular tradition has also given substance to Arthur as a possible occupant of the hillfort of South Cadbury in Somerset. It was the sixteenth-century traveller John Leland who recorded it as 'Camallate, sumtyme a famose town or castelle, upon a very torre or hille, wonderfully enstrengthened of nature . . . The people can telle nothing ther but that they have hard say that Arture much resortid to Camallate.' The excavations of 1966–70 revealed signs of a timber hall and of a stone-and-timber fortification of a standard befitting a powerful chieftain

Tintagel has a strong claim as the site of a palace of a British prince of Arthurian date.

or king. The discovery of Mediterranean ware of the same types as at Tintagel enabled a fairly precise dating to the closing decades of the fifth century, absolutely spot on for the Arthurian chronology. The majestic outlook of South Cadbury and the sense of security it offers in such a commanding location made it a perfect base for settlement since the Neolithic period. The steep climb up to the ramparts is rewarded, on a fine day, by some of the best views in the West Country.

Cornwall claims the site of Arthur's last and fatal battle at Camlann. About one mile to the north of Camelford, and some 200 yards north of the aptly named Slaughter Bridge, there lies a massive stone by the River Camel. The Latin inscription was once thought to contain the name of Arthur, and although this has now been disproved,

The inscribed stone lying by the banks of the Camel River near Slaughter Bridge has been popularly interpreted as marking the spot where Arthur received his fatal wound in battle.

Dozmary Pool on Bodmin Moor is the strongest contender for the scene in Arthurian legend where an arm emerges from the waters to clasp the sword Excalibur and draws it down into the depths of the lake. Another possible location is Loe Pool near Helston in Cornwall.

The Sancreed Cross is a fine example of the tall, round-headed Cornish type.

the stone has somehow been indelibly stamped with the seal of Arthurian legend as marking the place where Arthur fell after receiving his mortal wound from Mordred. The subsequent episode in the tale which involved the casting of the sword Excalibur into a lake is contested between two Cornish locations, Dozmary Pool on Bodmin Moor and Loe Pool by the coast near Helston. It was once believed that Dozmary Pool was so deep as to be bottomless, but it actually dried up in 1859 and was seen to be in reality quite shallow. Facts of this nature do nothing, however, to discourage the true believers; and Dozmary Pool is still generally known as the place where the mysterious arm rose from the waters to catch the sword reluctantly thrown by Bedivere and drew it with a flourish back below the surface of the lake.

Geoffrey of Monmouth had already established the Isle of Avalon as the last resting place of Arthur, but its actual location was not divulged. The question was to be settled in the most decisive manner by the monks of Glastonbury in 1190 when they announced that they had found the bones of Arthur and Guinevere following a tip-off relayed to Henry II by an anonymous Celtic source. It has been pointed out that Glastonbury was short of funds following a fire in 1184 which necessitated a complete rebuilding, so the discovery of the Arthurian relics could not have come at a better time with their potential to attract the lucrative pilgrimage traffic as well as other donations to pay for the programme of works. Needless to say, the lead cross which identified the occupant of the tomb to be Arthur with its Latin inscription has in the meantime mysteriously disappeared and survives only as a drawing made by William Camden and published in 1607. As for the bones of Arthur and Guinevere, they were eventually placed in 1278 in a prestigious tomb of black marble in front of the high altar at Glastonbury Abbey; but the iconoclasm of the Dissolution probably saw to their destruction for there is no trace of them today. The spot where the monks allegedly dug up the original coffin has been excavated and found to contain stone slabs commensurate with an earlier burial of some importance. This is perhaps the nearest we can come to approaching the real Arthur: an empty grave, a coffin and a cross that have been spirited away.

After the demise of Arthur, the Saxon invaders made a fitful but remorseless progress westwards, taking almost 300 years to overwhelm Dumnonia. The great linear earthwork of the Wansdyke in Wiltshire did not detain them for long; but the Durotriges of Dorset, the custodians of the Cerne Giant, held out for a long time until the early sixth century behind the protective shield of the Bokerley Dyke, later falling back to another earthwork known as Combs Ditch; but by the middle of the seventh century the Saxons had taken the area around Dorchester. The survival of a British or Celtic identity in Dorset is attested by the memorial inscriptions from the seventh to ninth centuries to be found in the church of St Mary in Wareham. However, the Saxons were more efficient in leaving their imprint on both the landscape and the map: over 75 per cent of Dorset place-names are Saxon, although most of the rivers still bear names of Celtic derivation. There is still much uncertainty as to the extent the Britons were expelled or simply fled from their lands. Modern views tend to stress integration and cohabitation of the rival communities, but there remains the mass exodus of Celtic folk from Cornwall to Brittany in the fifth century to be accounted for. Indeed, it was the great influx of Britons into Armorica which caused that part of Gaul to be renamed as Britannia, subsequently Bretagne in French. The lack of Celtic place-names in Devon – less than 1 per cent – has been interpreted as a sign that the Celts had moved further west into Cornwall in advance of the Saxon settlement, thus presenting the newcomers with an empty land. But to compound the mystery and confusion, there is a corresponding lack of Saxon remains in Devon.

If the take-over was at least partly peaceful, there were also a number of battles, which, one by one, reversed the advantage gained by Arthur at Badon. The defeat at Dyrham in Wiltshire in AD 577 drove a wedge between the Britons of Wales and those of the West Country. In AD 682 the West Saxon king, Centwine, 'drove the Britons [of Devon and west Somerset] as far as the sea'. Cornwall held out until the early ninth century, when defeated by Egbert; and it was not until AD 938 that Athelstan finally subdued the western extremity of the old realm of Dumnonia. Some of the Cornish leaders during these centuries under the growing shadow of the Saxons are recorded on memorial stones such as that to Doniert, possibly a ninth century King of Cornwall, and the famous Tristan Stone of the mid-sixth century discovered near the old fortifications of Castle Dore, which were re-occupied in the fifth century and showed traces of timber halls that may have been the 'palace' of King Mark of Cornwall. The Tristan Stone has now been moved to a place on the main road just north of Fowey, where it stands rather oddly, suggesting a megalithic bus stop.

The Arthurian legend remains the principal beacon to light the gloom of those centuries in the Celtic west, but the stark picture of Christians versus pagans does not typify the Dark Ages as a whole. The Saxons themselves converted to Christianity in the aftermath of Augustine's mission of AD 597, so that a reconciliation between the opposing sides must have been eased. Following the Celtic saints of earlier days, the West Country now received the first of a new line of Saxon saints. St Boniface from Crediton moved to Exeter in around AD 685 before embarking on his missionary activities in Germany. In AD 705 St Aldhelm was appointed first Bishop of Sherborne by Ine, King of the West Saxons. Under Athelstan, the first Saxon bishopric in Cornwall was founded at St Germans, but by a wise act of political and religious diplomacy, the Cornish Conan was appointed bishop. It was Athelstan who established the Tamar as a dividing line – if not a full political frontier – which gave the Britons of Cornwall that small degree of autonomy which they have jealously conserved to this day, maintaining the last flame in England of the old Celtic spirit.

The famous Bodmin Font is an artistic tour de force *of Norman carving in stone.*

Church and Chapel

Our vision of the English countryside, and in particular of the West Country, is of church towers and steeples studding the landscape, forming anchorages around which the humbler dwellings of the villages and hamlets cluster for protection and reassurance. Almost every foundation defines the presence of a rural community going back at least to the centuries before the Norman Conquest when the ordering of the parishes in England was commenced. In the ancient Celtic realm of Cornwall, untouched by the Saxons until relatively late, the churches often stand on the earlier site of a monk's abode, a hermit's cell or a saint's retreat by a holy well, close to but not part of a settlement. Whether of Celtic or Saxon origin, the churches which arose over the centuries must have been familiar and comforting sights to countless generations labouring in the fields, for they served not just as spiritual and religious shrines but equally as centres of social and even business activities, assuming a dominance in the lives of the people which has no modern equivalent. Today the parish churches are maintained by ever dwindling congregations, and suffer competition not just from the plethora of chapels of various denominations but from a variety of secular distractions. Try, however, to imagine a village without its church, and it is clear that its days are far from numbered. The interest of many people may now be confined to the architectural details of Norman design, the Gothic phases of Early English, Decorated and Perpendicular, as well as the craftsmanship of rood screens, carved bench ends, medieval stained glass and roof beams, but parish churches mean much more than the sum of their artistic merits; they are the essential element which holds together the fabric of the landscape and human society.

The existence of pre-Norman churches in the West Country is well attested, but the physical traces are scant, most churches having been rebuilt more than once on top of their original foundations. The Roman tiles re-used in the Dorset church at Whitechurch Canonicorum were probably quarried from the ruins of a secular building in the vicinity. This church is also noted for its unique shrine, which actually contains the bones of its patron St Wite. Although often even the foundations of the Celtic and Saxon churches have been erased below ground by the radical rebuilding of the Normans, the square-ended Celtic chancel was to define the pattern of the typical parish church of later centuries, a distinct English preference as opposed to the round apse of France.

There is a thin scattering of Saxon remains mainly in the east of the region. St Martin, Wareham in Dorset, has several Saxon features such as the 'long-and-short' work of the quoins; and its tall, narrow, square tower is typically Saxon, although some experts date it to the sixteenth-century rebuilding. The entire nave of St Michael, Winterbourne Steepleton in Dorset is Saxon; and outside the south aisle of the church may be found a piece of tenth-century sculpture of tremendous artistry depicting a flying angel. It is by such fragments of sculpture rather than through works of architecture that we can understand the contribution of the Saxons in the West Country. Even of Alfred the Great's church at Athelney in Somerset of 878 there is now no known trace. At Colerne in Wiltshire and Colyton in Devon there are particularly fine fragments of Saxon

St Laurence, Bradford-on-Avon, is one of the best preserved Saxon churches in the country.

crosses. The cross shaft at Codford St Peter in Wiltshire is adorned with a unique portrayal of a man holding a branch aloft in one hand and a mallet in the other, superbly incised and generally dated to the ninth century. Also in Wiltshire, in the church of St John Baptist, Inglesham, there is a famous Saxon carving of the Madonna and Child under the protective hand of God. This sculpture shows a fine and touching sensitivity of a kind that was soon to be banished by the crude but powerful carvings of the Normans.

Were it not for the inspired detective work of a nineteeth-century Wiltshire cleric, the existence of one of the most important Saxon churches in England as a whole might have escaped detection. Canon Jones of Bradford-on-Avon had already suspected an ancient church to be lurking within a curious structure in his parish which had been subdivided into a three-storey cottage and a schoolroom and further disguised by the proximity of other buildings as well as by a protective covering of ivy. Then in 1871 he came across a reference in the *Gesta Pontificum* of William of Malmesbury *c.* 1125: 'to this day at that place [Bradford-on-Avon] there exists a little church (*ecclesiola*) which Aldhelm is said to have built to the name of the most blessed Laurence.' Canon Jones rapidly surmised that he knew the location of the *ecclesiola* in question.

Following the identification of the Saxon church of St Laurence in Bradford-on-Avon as an original foundation of the very early eighth century, the building was acquired and restored. Opinion is now divided as to the dating of the church, ranging from the eighth to the tenth centuries, with the later date finding increasing support. Quite remarkably for a building of such antiquity it represents seemingly just a single construction phase with no subsequent alteration. The church retains the original narrow width (3 ft 6 in) of the chancel arch which rises to the grand height of 9 ft 8 in. The arches of the characteristic side chambers known as the 'porticus' are a mere 3 ft in width. High up on the east wall of the nave are two angels, floating horizontally, obviously close relatives of the one at the church of Winterbourne Steepleton. At the church of St Laurence the square-ended chancel is firmly English in character. The arcading, created after the construction of the building, was actually cut out of the masonry in bold relief. By any standards the church of St Laurence, Bradford-on-Avon, is an outstanding example of sophisticated design, which belies its age of at least a thousand years.

Under the Normans the parish church was to undergo a rapid and vigorous development. Once the new lords of the land had secured themselves behind the defences of the 'motte-and-bailey', a great rebuilding was commenced. Celtic chapels and Saxon churches gave way to a new generation of solid, well-crafted structures of smoothly hewn masonry designed to convey the power and permanence not just of Jesus Christ but also of the Norman occupiers. The Saxons had employed the same round arch of the Romanesque style but there the similarity with the Normans ceased. Instead of walls of rubble, great blocks of tailored stone were heaped up. Sturdy, square central towers at the crossing of nave, transepts and chancel gave the Norman parish church its characteristic martial aspect. The technology of the castle applied to the church may be seen at St Nicholas, Worth Matravers, in Dorset and at St Mary, Mortehoe, in Devon which inspired the lines by Tennyson: 'that tower of strength which stood four-square to all the winds that blew'.

We tend to think of the Normans, on account of their language, as a French phenomenon, but their original Norse roots are there for all to see in the mouldings and carvings with which they adorned those powerful round arches of their churches. At All Saints, Lullington in Somerset, the north door presents us with an outer moulding of grotesque animal heads, and the

The Norman font at Altarnun, Cornwall, is a powerful piece of figurative sculpture.

The church at Altarnum shows several characteristic Cornish features, from the Norman font and carved bench ends to the pleasing wagon-roof construction.

The Priory Church of Stogursey, Somerset, (left) *contains a chancel arch of Norman date.*

tympanum shows two wild beasts devouring the Tree of Life, imagery which clearly borrows much from the violence of Norse mythology. Within the nave of St Morwenna at Morwenstow in Cornwall, the central arch of the north aisle arcade provides a perch for a gallery of weird faces, some twenty-six in all, positioned at regular intervals of a few inches, like archers spaced out along a battlement. Six of them are reasonable likenesses of bearded men but the rest portray sinister, bird-like creatures with staring eyes and huge beaks which protrude menacingly. This is a world away from the tender, almost domestic style of Anglo-Saxon sculpture. The frightening motifs of Norman carving are here, as elsewhere, intensified by the fierce vigour of deeply incised chevrons or zig-zag patterns which resemble the teeth of a saw, so that to walk through some Norman doorways is like entering the jaws of a wild beast. The aim may have been to ward off evil but the church-goers were probably suitably intimidated as well. The total effect must have been truly awesome when one considers that Norman carvings were originally decorated with the most garish colours.

While so much Norman work has been lost in a series of rebuildings throughout the Middle Ages, a surprising number of Norman fonts have survived, especially in Cornwall, where some 111 are recorded. These are mostly of various abstract designs but several are masterpieces of figurative art. The famous font in the church of St Petroc, Bodmin, is acknowledged as the best of its type in the county. A deep bowl rests in fact on a squat central shaft, but it appears to be supported by four slender columns at the corners surmounted by busts of angels impassively keeping watch. An even more striking example of four faces resolutely protecting the baptismal water from any dark forces that may be lurking is to be found in the church of St Nonna in Altarnun on the fringe of Bodmin Moor. The primitive bearded faces appear to show vestiges of the colouring as it was originally intended.

The transition from the round arch of the Normans to the pointed arch of Gothic architecture may better be followed in cathedrals rather than in parish churches. The Early English phase of Gothic in the thirteenth century made only occasional appearances at parish level, largely because the building programme of the Normans from about 1150 to 1250 had been so comprehensive and efficient. The graceful purity of the style can, however, be sampled at St Mary, Potterne, and St Mary, Bishops Cannings, both in Wiltshire, but these were of special significance at the time, belonging to the Chapter of Salisbury. Quite apart from the new lightness and elegance of the pointed arch by contrast to the heavy round arch of the Normans, there was a growing refinement in carving as well. The crude blows of the axe gave way to the delicate strokes of the chisel at the same time as the fearsome images of the Normans were followed by homelier, more earth-bound evocations of a medieval imagination that did not seek to exclude the humour of everyday life from even the most exalted of structures dedicated to the worship of God.

As churches needed to be enlarged to accommodate the growing population of the villages, so new aisles were added and the latest style of Gothic might be attached to the original building until it became smothered by such accretions. The purity of Early English gave way in the first half of the fourteenth century to the more elaborate, hence Decorated period. St Mary Redcliffe in Bristol displays some of the best examples of the style. Indeed, its north porch, of *c.* 1320–30, shows just how apt the term 'Decorated' really is to describe this style, the complete antithesis to the chaste simplicity of Early English. The doorway to the hexagonal north porch is framed by a quasi-oriental design of great intricacy, fanciful curves and richness of detail. The walls are punctuated by can-

The carved wooden roof of the church at Westonzoyland is one of the glories of Somerset.

opied niches under nodding ogee arches. It was in the chamber above this exotic porch that the ill-fated boy-poet Chatterton spent several days poring over medieval manuscripts. The church of St Mary at Ottery St Mary in Devon is a more complete realisation of the Decorated style, far too grand for a simple parish church since it was built by Bishop Grandison of Exeter who acquired the manor of Ottery St Mary in 1335. The stone vaults with their flowing rib pattern show that stylistic invention has taken over from the cult of austerity.

This delightful phase of Gothic was cut short in 1348 by the horrors of the Black Death. Although the whole of England was affected, the West Country was particularly hard hit. In fact, it was almost certainly through a ship calling at the Dorset port of Melcombe Regis in the summer of that fateful year that the bubonic plague was brought ashore by the fleas of the black rat. As life recovered during the second half of the fourteenth century the prosperity of the wool industry created an ever-increasing surplus of wealth which was lavished on the parish churches of the wool-producing counties. This boom coincided with the

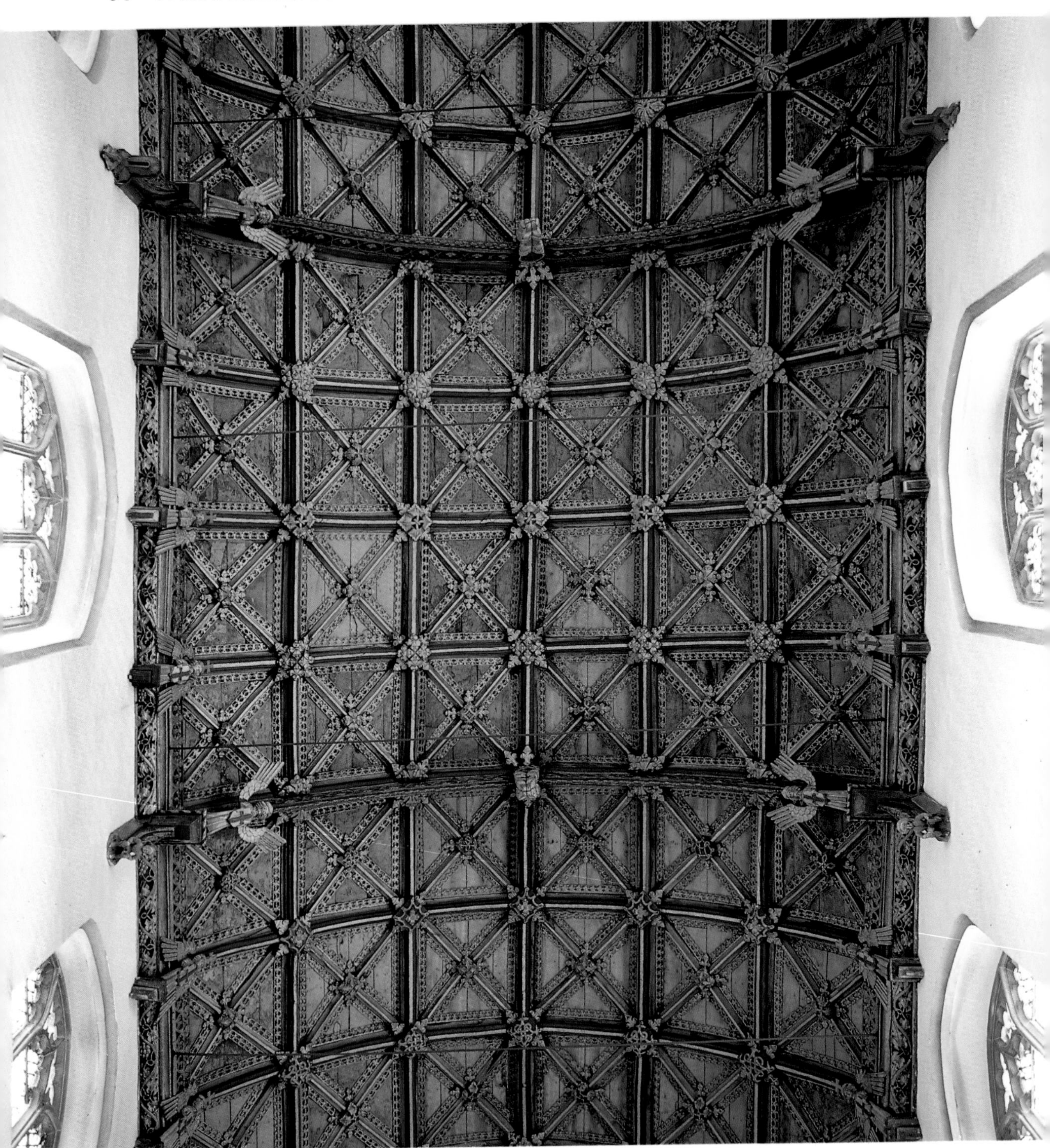

The parish church of Cullompton in Devon boasts one of the most elegant wagon-roofs in the West Country. The church also contains the Lane Aisle, built by a wealthy clothier.

The oak roof of the church at Bere Regis, Dorset, dates back to the fifteenth century and was probably the gift of Cardinal Morton. Notable among the wealth of decoration are the full-length carved figures representing the Twelve Apostles.

A brave attempt to coax carving out of tough Cornish granite at Launceston, Cornwall.

final phase of Gothic, known as Perpendicular from its stress on vertical lines as well as shallow arches, wide expanses of glass, noble towers and beautifully carved timber roofs which represent the most glorious era in the church architecture of the West Country. In quantity as well as quality Perpendicular became the dominant style of the region, so energetic was the rebuilding that occurred at this time.

The vivacity and variety of timber roofs to be found in the West Country suggest that the carpenters were at last responding to the ascendancy of the masons who were now erecting those magnificent pinnacled towers with which Somerset churches are so generously endowed. It is a thrill to enter a parish church such as St Mary, Weston Zoyland in Somerset, and to feel oneself almost physically drawn up to the beams by the splendour of the carved angels whose wings appear to be carrying the entire roof. The experience may be repeated at the church of St Cuthbert in Wells, whose roof was restored in 1963 and is resplendent with colour once more. Another polychromatic feast for the eyes awaits in St John Baptist, Bere Regis in Dorset. The magnificent oak roof, which features full-length figures of the twelve apostles, is thought to have been the gift of Cardinal Morton (1420–1500), Archbishop of Canterbury. All Saints, Martock, in Somerset, has a roof full of angels, breathtaking in the scale and conception of the work, which bears the date 1513. Closer inspection of the west end of the roof reveals, however, that wool money was after all a finite resource, for the size and quality of the angelic host falls away rapidly. Evidently, the budget was overspent and the carvers were not willing or able to continue the same high standard throughout. The wagon or cradle-roof was a speciality of the West Country. The lofty example of St Peter and St Paul in Shepton Mallet has been acclaimed as the most glorious in all England, but no account should omit the splendid wagon-roof of St Andrew, Cullompton in Devon, or even that of All Saints, Selworthy in Somerset. More modest specimens of the genre, which makes sparing use of timber, are to be found especially in Cornwall, such as that in the church of St Nonna, Altarnun.

The generosity of rich benefactors was often astounding, as was the case at St Andrew, Cullompton, where John Lane, a clothier of the town, financed a complete aisle which is a marvel of fan-vaulting of a quality to match that of the Henry VII Chapel at Westminster Abbey. Only here it is not royalty that is commemorated but the success of an ordinary wool merchant, as may be seen from the angels bearing emblems of sheep-shears, and carvings of Tudor men of commerce holding bolts of cloth or long scrolls likely to contain the accounts of their lucrative dealings. Lane's aisle was possibly built in response to the chapel endowed by his friend and rival John Greenway at St Peters, Tiverton in 1517. This chantry chapel of dazzling white stone displays a frieze of stylised ocean waves carrying an entire fleet of armed merchant ships which transported the exports of wool and the imports of wine and spices. It was a businessman, William Canynge, who completed the Perpendicular work at St Mary Redcliffe in Bristol, a veritable cathedral among parish churches, which Elizabeth I described as 'the fairest, goodliest, and most famous parish church in England'. Another extravagant personal gesture was the rebuilding of St Mary Magdalene, Launceston in Cornwall, in 1511–24 by Sir Henry Trecarrel. Not to be outdone by

Hungerford effigies repose in the chapel of Farleigh Hungerford Castle in Somerset.

This chapel at St Peters, Tiverton in Devon, was endowed by the local businessman John Greenway. The ships which helped make his fortune in the wool trade are boldly carved.

The elegant tower of St Mary Magdalene, Taunton, (right) *is generally acclaimed as the grandest expression of Somerset's magnificent heritage of church architecture.*

Littlecote, Wiltshire, contains a unique Cromwellian chapel of the new auditory type.

anyone, he insisted that the exterior of the church be adorned with carvings, even though the material to be carved was hard, obdurate granite. Nevertheless, the crude work is strangely powerful and impressive.

Such lavish acts speak of a growing concern on the part of individuals for the salvation of their souls in the life to come. The same undercurrent of anxiety may be deduced from the numerous funeral monuments and the increasingly naturalistic portrayal of the effigies which are crammed into churches and chapels all over the region. It is a moving experience to encounter the West Country gentry in deathly repose, notably Sir John Popham in St John Baptist, Wellington in Somerset, the St Johns and Mompessons at St Mary, Lydiard Tregoze in Wiltshire, the Bluetts in the parish church of Holcombe Rogus in Devon and the Hungerfords in the Chapel of St Leonard within the walls of Farleigh Hungerford Castle in Somerset.

Towards the end of the Middle Ages growing emphasis on the sermon was already leading to the installation of fixed seating, notably in the form of box-pews whose carved bench-ends are another glory of the West Country. Those at St Michael, Brent Knoll in Somerset, show the unexpected inventiveness and humour to be found. Here an abbot is portrayed as a fox, while the monks have the heads of pigs in a series of bench-ends which present a satirical parable which can only be understood now in broad terms. Other jewels among the bench-ends are to be encountered in the church of East Budleigh in Devon, while the church of St Senner at Zennor, Cornwall, has conserved the wonderful portrayal of a seductive mermaid. Such images, along with the religious statues and stained glass, suffered untold damage during the Reformation of the sixteenth century and the Puritan excesses of the seventeenth. Church building virtually ground to a halt for a hundred years from about the middle of the sixteenth century. Thus it was against the general trend that St Mary, Croscombe, in Somerset acquired its remarkable Jacobean interior of pews and gallery dominated by the lofty pulpit under its ornate sounding board. It is also an exceedingly rare thing to come across a Cromwellian-style chapel, as has been preserved intact within the great house of Littlecote in Wiltshire for over three hundred years. This is a unique survival of Cromwellian England, an uncompromising variant of the auditory layout where the preacher's sermon has ousted the mystery of the Mass as the central event, and the pulpit has replaced the altar as the focal point. The box-type pews in the Littlecote Chapel were cunningly designed so that anyone who slouched would slide off the narrow benches, a crude but effective device to prevent the congregation falling asleep or quite literally 'dropping off' during the lengthy sermons.

The auditory structure characterised the next generation of chapels and places of worship built by the Dissenters or Nonconformists such as the Quakers, Baptists and Methodists, whose message was so warmly received in the West Country. Loughwood, one of the earliest meeting houses of the Baptists, lies in a secluded spot near Dalwood, four miles west of Axminster. At first Baptist meetings were held in barns, private houses or even the open countryside to avoid detection during the time when Nonconformism was prohibited. In the years following the Restoration of the Monarchy in 1660 until the Toleration Act of 1688 the penalties and risks in attending such meetings were particularly harsh. Consequently, secrecy and discretion dictated the site of meeting houses such as Loughwood, which in the seventeenth century would have been surrounded by a thick forest cover. Members often had to travel long distances to attend, so provision was made for retiring rooms beneath the gallery and for basic cooking facilities. First records of the Loughwood Meeting House extend back to 1653, and the present structure dates substantially from the seventeenth century. From the outside the only clue to the non-secular function of the building, which could be taken for a schoolhouse, is the slight Gothic arch of the windows. Architectural camouflage was dictated not only out of discretion but also because the Nonconformists wished to avoid the Anglican symbolism of the parish churches with their towers, steeples, transepts, chancel and imagery. The interior of Loughwood Meeting House, which is essentially of very early eighteenth-century date, is wonderfully intact; its orderly austerity of pews of untreated pine against blank whitewashed walls forms a complete contrast to the complexities of Gothic style. The Christian place of worship has undergone a thorough demystification.

Another fine example of the type, built by the early Quakers in Cornwall, is the meeting house near Feock called sweetly Come-to-Good, not a genuine name but an apt phonetic rendering of the Cornish 'Cwn-ty-coit' meaning 'the combe by the dwelling in the wood'. This meeting house was built in 1710, just over a half a century since George Fox, the founder of the Religious Society of Friends, had visited Cornwall and ended up

The meeting house at Come-to-Good at Feock shows the austere but homely Quaker style, for the Nonconformists were anxious not to imitate the established church architecture.

The Baptists built their meeting house at Loughwood in Devon at the end of the seventeenth century. The spartan interior with its hard box pews is wonderfully preserved.

This Classical building at East Lulworth, Dorset, conceals England's first Roman Catholic church since the Reformation.

in one of the worst cells of Launceston Gaol, 'a nasty, stinking place, where they said few people came out alive; where they used to put witches and murderers, before their execution; where the prisoners' excrements had not been carried out for scores of years as it was said'. It was from such degrading conditions that George Fox penned one of his most inspirational messages. He survived the ghastly experience and went on to begin in person Cornwall's first monthly meeting of Quakers held in 1688 near St Austell.

In Bristol there is a miraculous survival of John Wesley's early years as a Methodist preacher, located right in the middle of a heavily bombed and redeveloped part of the city centre. The New Room, as it is called, is the oldest Methodist church in the world. The house was purchased by John Wesley in 1739 and enlarged in 1748 to accommodate both the meetings and the minister's family in an apartment above. By means of a cleverly designed octagonal lantern it was possible for those in the rooms above to both see and hear the preacher in the room below. It was from the New Room at Bristol that John Wesley embarked on his numerous journeys around the West Country. The voice of Wesleyan Methodism was received with particular fervour by the tinners of Cornwall. Wesley's favourite preaching place in the county was in a surface depression caused by the falling-in of old mine workings at Gwennap Pit near Redruth, which he affectionately called 'my amphitheatre'. Crowds of up to 20,000 would converge on Gwennap Pit for Wesley's sermons.

Wesley's special place in the hearts of the people of Cornwall, where he made as many as thirty-two visits between 1743–89, is reflected in the rash of methodist chapels that were built in the towns and villages of the county during the nineteenth century, quite enough to outnumber the churches founded by the Celtic saints. The architecture of nineteenth-century Methodism, sadly lacking in imagination, may be seen with depressing regularity and cannot compare with the homely simplicity of the early 'prattling boxes' as the Nonconformist chapels were described by the Mayor of Bristol in 1664. Nor was the message of Methodism without its critics. The eccentric Reverend Hawker of Morwenstow was unequivocal: 'With my last breath I protest that the man Wesley corrupted and depraved instead of improving the West of England, indeed all the land. He found the miners and fishermen an upstanding, rollicking, courageous people. He left them a downlooking, lying, selfish-hearted throng.' Nevertheless, it has been argued that in the nineteenth century Methodism had become the established Church of Cornwall.

It was also in the West Country that the first Roman Catholic church to be built in England since the Reformation was erected in 1786–7. The story behind this curious building near Lulworth Castle in Dorset, which resembles a garden temple in a picturesque landscape, is that George III granted Thomas Weld permission to build his church on the strict condition that its identity should be disguised. And so St Mary (R.C.) at East Lulworth still appears today as one of those Classical follies so beloved of that time. Classical forms dominated the Anglican church architecture of the eighteenth century in the West Country as elsewhere. The Gothic Revival of the nineteenth left many marks; and among the designs of the front-rank exponents of the genre are the parish churches of All Saints, Babbacombe in Devon, by Butterfield and the quite remarkable St James, Kingston in Dorset, by Street. The latter was a product of lavish personal patronage, the entire financing having been provided by the third Earl of Eldon. It can be seen for miles and totally dominates its relatively undersized village. Equally out of context is the extravaganza of the church of St Mary and St Nicholas at Wilton in Wiltshire, a bold nineteenth-century rendering of the Lombardic style. Such artificial, although impressive, works point to the complete break with the regional church architecture of the past that occurred in the West Country long before the dawn of the twentieth century.

Street's grand new church at Kingston, Dorset.

Delicately carved capitals at Wells Cathedral add a human touch to the Gothic architecture.

The Building of Cathedrals

The cathedrals of the West Country – Bristol, Exeter, Salisbury, Truro and Wells – all now assume an air of permanence at the heart of their respective cities as if their pre-eminence derives from an antiquity beyond human reach and recall. Even the late nineteenth-century cathedral of Truro sits no less self-confidently than the others, its cathedral status giving it a *gravitas* as of the most ancient lineage, which belies its surprisingly recent creation in 1876. However, there is no divine right of cathedrals to be cathedrals; there is nothing intrinsically sacred about the masonry or the ground upon which they sit. Instead, they derive their authority and title from their role as seat (from the Latin '*cathedram*') of the bishop appointed to a particular see. Like all else in the course of history the definition of the dioceses has fluctuated along with political and socio-economic movements as well as in line with the ambitions and predilections of individual clerics. Thus cathedrals can come and go, vulnerable not just as physical structures but also as embodiments of ecclesiastical power.

Sherborne has experienced, perhaps more than any other place in the region, the vicissitudes occasioned by the evolving organisation of the Church of England. It is well known that the present parish church of Sherborne was once a prosperous abbey of the Benedictine order, but before that Sherborne had already served as a cathedral for as long as 370 years. Its career as a seat of a bishop goes back to the year 705 when the great St Aldhelm was appointed to the diocese of Sherborne created by King Ine of Wessex. With the westward advance of the Saxons, Winchester was no longer a convenient diocesan centre for the newly acquired territories in the south-west, so Sherborne received its chance. As the Saxons made further inroads into the ancient kingdom of Dumnonia, so Sherborne's holy see expanded apace. By the end of the ninth century the Bishops of Sherborne were spiritual lords of a diocese which stretched west from the borders of Wiltshire to comprise the counties of Dorset, Somerset, Devon and Cornwall. This vast area was subdivided in 909 with the establishment of new sees at Wells for Somerset and at Crediton for Devon and Cornwall. In 926 Athelstan transferred the see of Cornwall to St Germans where it remained for just over a century until 1043 when it passed back to Crediton. In 1050 it was the turn of Crediton to lose its cathedral status when Bishop Leofric made Exeter the seat of the bishopric covering Devon and Cornwall. Thus by the time of the Norman Conquest St Germans and Crediton had already seen an end to their episcopal aspirations. Sherborne was soon to follow, for it was removed from the ranks of English cathedral cities in 1075. All that remains today of what was once virtually the cathedral to the entire West Country is a blocked Saxon doorway in the west wall of Sherborne Abbey. This was part of Bishop Alfwold's 'New Cathedral' of *c.* 1050, the last of three Saxon building phases prior to the complete rebuilding in the twelfth century by the Norman founders of the Benedictine abbey. It is a modest but poignant relic of Sherborne's erstwhile predominance in the religious affairs of the region.

The demise of the cathedral at Sherborne was caused by an order of the Council of London in 1075 which decreed that bishoprics should be translated, where necessary, from rural to more populated centres. So it happened that the bishopric was removed to the unlikely location of Old Sarum in Wiltshire, an Iron Age hillfort which had

The outline of the original cathedrals at Old Sarum, Wiltshire, remain visible in the grass.

been reoccupied by the Saxons as a convenient stronghold against raids by the Vikings. A small but thriving township had grown up within the ramparts which was joined soon after the Conquest by a Norman motte-and-bailey castle. It is strange, when viewed from our present perspective, to see Old Sarum as a greater centre of population than Sherborne. William of Malmesbury, writing in the twelfth century, thought so too, describing Old Sarum as 'a castle rather than a city, an unknown place'.

As it happened, the location of a bishop's seat at Old Sarum turned out to be an ill-fated venture from the start. The first cathedral was largely destroyed by a storm in 1092 just five days after its consecration in the name of the Blessed Virgin. The outline of its round apse of Romanesque tradition can still be seen enclosed within the exposed foundations of the successor cathedral's longer, square-ended chancel. This building, completed by Bishop Roger early in the twelfth century, was of such excellent masonry that William of Malmesbury thought it might have been carved out of just one piece of stone. Architectural excellence was not enough, however, to keep the clerics content. The condominium with the castle, which also controlled access to the town, became increasingly fraught after the downfall and death of Bishop Roger in 1139. Henceforth the clergy and the soldiery were hostile neighbours cooped up together. On one occasion in 1217 the Dean and clergy found themselves locked out of Old Sarum after a Rogationtide procession on the pretext that the gate had to be kept shut because of the danger of an imminent attack by the Germans. A campaign to have the cathedral removed to Salisbury was at last successful in 1219 when Pope Honorius III issued the necessary Bull which summarised the complaints about Old Sarum:

> Situated within a castle, the church is subject to such inconvenience that the clergy cannot stay there without danger to their persons. The church is exposed to such winds that those celebrating the divine offices can hardly hear each other speak. The fabric is so ruinous that it is a constant danger to the congregation which has dwindled to such an extent that it is hardly able to provide for the repair of the roofs, which are constantly damaged by the winds. Water is so scarce that it has to be bought at a high price, and access to it is not to be had without the governor's permission. People wishing to visit the cathedral are often prevented by guards from the garrison. Housing is insufficient for the clergy who are therefore forced to buy houses from laymen. The whiteness of the chalk causes blindness.

Following the successful conclusion of his highly professional lobbying of the Pope, Bishop Richard Poore was able to lead his flock from the glaring, windswept and waterless hill of Old Sarum to what must have seemed like a promised land of meadows watered by the Rivers Avon, Nadder and Bourne. The new cathedral of Salisbury was to arise quite literally on a green-field site. Building was commenced in 1220 and completed by about 1360 in the austerely elegant Early English phase of Gothic. Whereas most other English cathedrals were being rebuilt piecemeal throughout the Middle Ages and thus acquired traces of the succession of architectural styles, Salisbury arose at a phenomenal rate in the one style. By 1280 it was already complete with the exception of the tower and spire. The work so far had consumed 60,000 tons of Chilmark stone quarried twelve miles to the west of the city as well as 12,000 tons of Purbeck marble from the mines at Downshay. The redundant cathedral at Old Sarum was demolished in about 1331 and its stone was used for the great wall built around the Close at that time.

Given the stylistic and aesthetic unity of Salisbury Cathedral which gives the impression of a grand design, it comes as a surprise to discover that the tower and spire were built as an entirely separate phase commenced some fifty years after the rest of the building, their construction being dated to *c.* 1330–60. Furthermore, there is every indication that the original structure was not designed to support the great weight of the tower and spire because extra buttressing was required to contain the thrust caused by the 6,400 tons of additional material above the level of the lantern. The massive bulk of the central part of Salisbury Cathedral rests on four piers which extend not more than 4 ft below the ground. Stability is aided by the natural layer of flint gravel, but even so there has occurred a declination of 29½ in in the alignment of the spire, which has happily remained constant since it was measured by Sir Christopher Wren over 300 years ago.

Salisbury's spire, despite its lean, may still be acclaimed as a miracle of construction

The cloisters of Salisbury Cathedral, built in the 1270s, are the largest in England. Their magnificent proportions are enhanced by elegant traceried arcades, a textbook example of the Decorated phase of Gothic architecture.

The west front of Salisbury Cathedral was heavily restored during the Victorian period.

and engineering in stone. For the first 20 ft of the 180 ft-high spire the stone is 2 ft thick. After this the outer skin of the octagonal spire thins to just 8 in, which is further reduced in places by carved decorations to an alarming 2 to 3 in. This literal *tour de force* of masonic audacity is held in place by a cunningly contrived timber scaffolding within the spire, of which more than three quarters is still of the original wood. Iron brackets fitted to the capstone permit the spire to be 'tightened up' when necessary. But even with such sophistication Salisbury's spire has created many problems over the centuries. As early as 1387 a record of a Chapter Meeting reveals that the spire was feared to be a threat to the entire cathedral. Today, some 600 years later, the great spire of Salisbury is once again the subject of an immensely expensive restoration programme. Although Salisbury without its spire may be unthinkable, the cathedral was originally built with a separate bell tower or *campanile*, which was sold off for scrap building materials in 1790 following the placing of an advertisement in the *Salisbury and Winchester Journal*. There is no trace today of the old bell tower except for the outline of its foundations which emerges as a ghostlike apparition in the grass during particularly dry periods.

The enduring majesty of Salisbury Cathedral has had many indignities to suffer, from drunks racing up the tower and urinating on those below them to the eighteenth-century 'improvements' of James Wyatt which included the destruction of most of what remained of the medieval glass, an incalculable loss. But it was Wyatt who gave us the fine, unobstructed view of the cathedral over a smooth expanse of lawn by removing a forest of gravestones. Gilbert Scott in the nineteenth century oversaw an extensive programme of restoration from 1860–75. Much of the statuary of the west front, not one of the glories of Salisbury, dates from this period. It is instructive to compare the stiff, conventional artistry of the Victorians with the animated carvings of medieval date to be found on the arches of the arcade of the Chapter House. These spirited portraits, albeit over-restored in the nineteenth century, provide a fascinating counterpoint to the perfection of Salisbury which some have found cold in its austerity.

If Salisbury represents the prime example of stylistic unity, then Wells provides almost the complete menu of Gothic architecture. Early English characterises much of the west front and the central tower up to roof level. The upper two stages of the tower along with the Chapter House and Lady Chapel belong to the period of Decorated Gothic. Perpendicular makes a brief but effective appearance on the two west towers and in the reworking of the top of the central tower which acquired traceried parapets and a host of pinnacles and statues in canopied recesses. A fan vault, that hallmark of the Perpendicular, was introduced inside at the base of the tower. But to describe Wells Cathedral in this way is to suggest that its effect is fragmented; and it is, on the contrary, impressive just how well all the various parts come together.

Wells was begun *c.* 1180, that is forty years before Salisbury, and it was the first major building in England to make use of the pointed arch throughout. The only slight reference to Norman architecture is the zig-zag decoration on the north porch. In contrast to Salisbury, Wells experienced a much longer and more troubled building history. There was even a sudden break of activity during the building of the nave itself between 1209–13 which has left its mark in a slightly larger size of stone employed as well as in different cutting techniques when work was resumed. Wells is an object lesson in the truth that the great cathedral builders of the Middle Ages, despite the sophistication of their methods, had at times to proceed by trial and error as they encountered unforeseen constructional problems. In the case of Wells, as at Salisbury, the trouble was caused by the tower. In 1313 the ambitious plan to raise the central tower to twice the height allowed for in the original design triggered off a chain of events which were to have a dramatic effect on the internal appearance of the cathedral. As the tower went up, so it was noticed that the additional weight caused the two western piers to sink into the ground whereas the two eastern piers held firm. This produced a dislocation of 7 in at the top of the tower, hardly alarming by the standards of Pisa, but enough to call for urgent remedial action. The answer was found in the insertion of monumental scissor arches, erected *c.* 1338–48, whose function is to transfer some of the weight of the tower from the west to the east. Depending on one's opinion, the scissor arches of Wells may be described as an eyesore which literally turns soaring Gothic on its

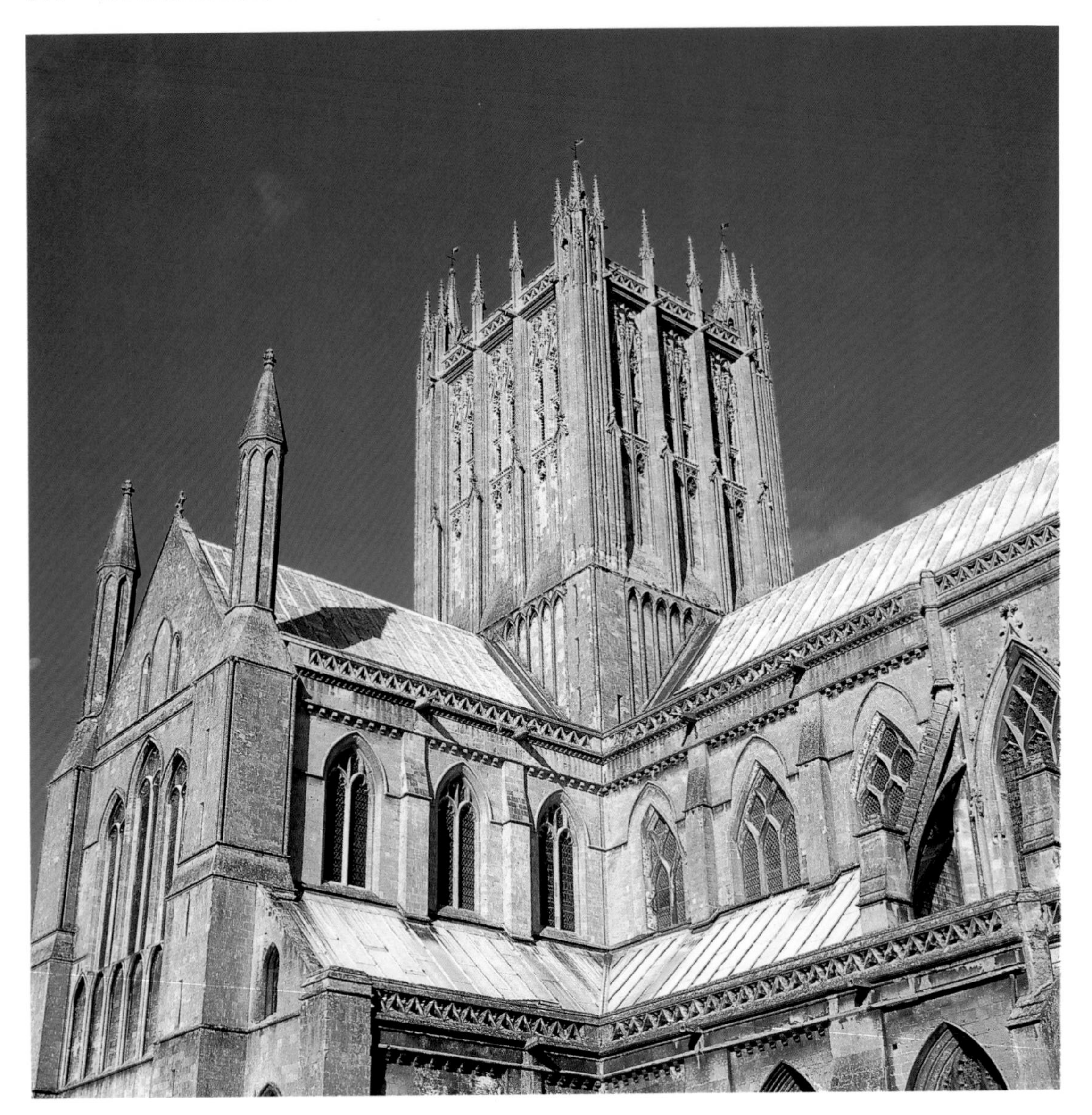

The central tower of Wells Cathedral displays a mixture of Early English in the lower level, Decorated in the upper stages, and with a crown of Perpendicular motifs.

The famous scissor arch at Wells (right) *was introduced to support the added weight of the central tower which was raised to a greater height than originally intended.*

The scratched effigy of Ralph of Shrewsbury, Bishop of Wells, creator of the Vicars Close.

head, or be acclaimed as a triumph of naked construction which is aesthetically pleasing on account of the bold and flamboyant design solution. Whatever one's verdict, there can be no denying that both the engineering and the masoncraft of the scissor arches at Wells are of the very highest order of merit.

Another highlight at Wells is the Chapter House, hailed by many as the finest in England. This is an exciting octagonal structure containing around its sides fifty-one canopied stalls adorned with a gallery of carved heads of kings, clerics and common folk under a spectacular tierceron vault of thirty-two ribs. The Chapter House is approached by a flight of steps which divides halfway up, with one flight continuing to the Chain Bridge and Vicar's Hall. From the foot of the stairs one has the impression of two glaciers of stone coming together from convergent valleys to continue down the slope as one consolidated mass. This is perhaps not an important part of the cathedral, but it is nonetheless an exciting spatial composition which is treasured by many. The staircase also bears signs of a major interruption in building when the money ran out, causing work to be abandoned in the 1240s and not resumed until 1286.

The west front of Wells is one of the undisputed glories of English cathedrals. The major part was completed by 1250, the two towers being added two centuries later. The entire west front was conceived as a huge screen for the display of a splendid array of medieval statuary. The original scheme allowed for 340 figures of sculpture, of which just under half were life-size or larger. Despite the depredations of time and destruction at the hands of the Puritans in the seventeenth century, enough survives to convey an idea of the majesty of the concept. This vast gallery contains a typical medieval mix of heavenly and profane subjects, ranging from the Apostles, angels, saints and the Resurrection to kings and knights in armour. King Solomon and the Queen of Sheba are there along with other Old Testament figures such as Noah, Adam and Eve. In a tympanum above the door is a portrayal of the Virgin and Child with angels in attendance. Originally, the carved detail was enhanced by paint of brilliant colours which aided recognition of the sculptural features when viewed from afar. There are holes in the stonework of the niches behind the angels, and it was through these that the choristers and vicars choral would sing on the days of the great church festivals. Particularly on Palm Sunday when the west door was used and there was a mighty throng of people the polychrome of the statuary must have had a dazzling effect on the onlookers, akin to a heavenly apparition, an experience heightened no doubt by the chanting which emanated as if by magic from the very fabric of the cathedral stone. The vicars choral who contributed in no small degree to the magnificence of such occasions were accommodated in the beautifully preserved street of houses to the north of the cathedral known as Vicars Close. This was the work of Bishop Ralph of Shrewsbury, who was also responsible for the fortifications and moat around the Bishop's Palace. At Wells as at Salisbury and Exeter the cathedrals were a pioneering influence in the evolving urbanism of the region.

Exeter is the third of the West Country's cathedrals of Old Foundation, as they have been known since the time of Henry VIII. Unlike the other two, Salisbury and Wells, Exeter goes back to a Norman foundation in 1050. The only obvious signs of this first phase are the two great towers built over the transepts, which although disguised by late fifteenth-century pinnacles and battlements in place of their previous pyramid-shaped spires, are still unmistakably Norman in their four-square solidity, blind interlaced arcading and zig-zag decoration. Exeter Cathedral was so extensively rebuilt during the Decorated period of the fourteenth century that the architectural handbooks usually cite it as the exponent *par excellence* of that particular style. The main excitement at Exeter is provided by the main vault which continues uninterrupted from the nave through the quire until it meets the east window. This 300-ft avenue of Gothic vaulting is the longest in existence anywhere. The lively springing of its stone ribs has been likened by more than one commentator to the effect of the crowns of palm trees. Where the palm fronds touch – to continue the simile – along the central ridge of the vault, the meeting points of the ribs are held together visually by a series of bosses, resplendent once more with gilt and colour since their recent restoration. Closer inspection of the bosses and the vaulting revealed the high standard achieved even at such a great height where all detail is lost to the naked eye down below in the nave. It was also

The west front of Exeter, bathed in late afternoon sun, is one of the most enchanting vistas to be experienced in the cathedral cities of England.

The view towards the west window of Exeter Cathedral (left) shows the palm-like effect of the spreading vault of the nave.

The Speke Chantry of 1517 in Exeter Cathedral represents a rich man's bid for salvation.

discovered that a variety of stones were used: Salcombe, Caen and Beer stone for the ribs, Ham Hill, Portland, Caen and Beer stone for the bosses. Hundreds of masons' marks, delicately incised into the stone and totally invisible from the ground, indicate the work accomplished by each individual. These marks of personal identity, along with the carved portraits of masons, give a delightful human dimension to Gothic cathedrals which might otherwise be perceived as monuments dedicated entirely to other-worldly aspirations.

The west front of Exeter Cathedral, which has also been recently restored, is a less successful arrangement than that at Wells. Atmospheric pollution from the nineteenth century on, coupled with injudicious replacement of some of the original statues at the beginning of the twentieth century, when a variety of unsuitable stones were used, has detracted considerably from the artistic merit of the composition. The use of bolts to secure unstable figures and even of cement to consolidate crumbling surfaces has created a host of conservation problems. Paint once helped to protect the stonework; and tiny patches of the bright colours so beloved of the Middle Ages have been discovered. Brilliant hues of blue, red, orange, green and yellow once gave this façade a vibrant effect. But we should not be too mindful – here as elsewhere – of lost glories lest we overlook the beauties that are left to enjoy. The west front of Exeter Cathedral in the late afternoon when the sun lights up the stonework across the open expanse of lawn in the Close is still one of the most satisfying views to be had in any cathedral city.

Inside Exeter Cathedral there is a striking item of interest in the Bishop's Throne, a wooden structure which rises in tiers of pinnacles to a height of 57 ft, straddling the borderline between furniture and architecture. The extravagance of the design serves to underline not just the authority of medieval bishops but also the decisive role they played in the building of cathedrals. Such a man was John of Tours, Bishop of Wells from 1088, who took such a strong dislike to Wells that he transferred the see to Bath in 1091, where he proceeded to dismiss all the monks and to bring over his own preferred breed of civilised brethren from the Continent. The cathedral built by John of Tours at Bath around the beginning of the twelfth century was at the time one of the largest and most impressive in England. The present sixteenth-century Bath Abbey occupies only the area covered by the nave of this mighty cathedral which measured 90 ft wide by 350 ft in length. Today only a few scraps of masonry remain of Bath's lost cathedral. They are discernible only to the initiate, located as they are high up in the east wall of the Abbey. After the demise of John of Tours in 1122 Bath's status as a diocesan centre was hotly disputed by the canons at Wells, and a move back to that city occurred during the last decades of the twelfth century; but it was not until 1245 that the Pope finally legalised the situation and authorised the incumbent at Wells to adopt the title of Bishop of Bath and Wells, and so it has remained until this day.

Henry VIII, that despoiler of the monasteries, is less well known for the diocesan reforms which created six new sees in the 1540s. Thus it came about that the Augustinian abbey at Bristol was saved from destruction to become one of the most complex of cathedrals. There is superb Norman work in the Chapter House and the arch of the great gatehouse, but the most impressive feature at Bristol is the novel form of the hall-church built by the Augustinians which now constitutes the east end of the cathedral. The present nave was built in the nineteenth century by Street in direct emulation of the earlier work after an interruption of more than 300 years. Street also designed the west towers, but the rebuilding of the central tower was accomplished by Pearson in the 1890s.

It was also to Pearson that the honour fell of preparing the drawings for a new cathedral for Truro in the 1870s when the diocese of Cornwall was removed from Exeter and finally returned to Cornish soil. The style of Truro Cathedral is a Victorian version of Early English, but its spirit is more akin to the cathedrals of northern France, located in the heart of the city with shops and houses pressing hard on the lofty structure without the *cordon sanitaire* of a Close. It has been suggested that this French association in the youngest of the cathedrals of the West Country commemorates the Cornish saints of the Dark Ages who travelled between Brittany and Cornwall and kept alive the Christian tradition in the west when most of the island of Britain had relapsed into paganism.

Gothic arches open to the sky tell of the glory that once was Glastonbury Abbey.

Rise and Fall of the Monasteries

The early monasticism of the Dark Ages in the West Country sprang from the most ancient Christian tradition nurtured in the lands of the eastern Mediterranean, notably Egypt and Syria, and probably brought to the kingdom of Dumnonia via the maritime routes of western Gaul. This was in inspiration and practice a religious devotion born of the desert and of a deep longing to flee the vanities and temptations of human society. The ascetic and eremetical tendency is apparent in the legends of the Cornish saints, most typically in the case of St Neot who is supposed to have recited psalms for hours on end immersed up to his neck in cold water. The early monasteries are thus assumed to have been primarily places of refuge and withdrawal rather than centres of missionary teaching. Their actual locations in the West Country – now that Tintagel's monastic identity has been called in question – are subject to some speculation, but it is considered that Crantock, Padstow, Probus, Perranzabuloe, St Buryan and St Keverne as well as St Germans are the most likely candidates for foundation by the sixth and seventh centuries. The mid-seventh-century '*Vita Sancti Samsonis*' refers to St Samson's monastery by a cave; and there must have existed several other small, scattered communities along the Cornish coast.

Soon after King Cynegils of the West Saxons was baptised a Christian in 635, Saxon monasteries began to spring up in the lands occupied by the newcomers. There was already a minster as far west as Exeter by about 675. At Muchelney in Somerset Benedictine monks were, according to tradition, established during the reign of King Ine of Wessex (688–726), and a faint trace of the round Saxon apse of the original church has been discovered among the ruined foundations of the twelfth-century rebuilding. Malmesbury Abbey claims to have been founded as early as 676, by St Aldhelm. In the ninth century Alfred the Great sponsored a monastic house at Athelney as well as the Benedictine Shaftesbury Abbey for nuns, consecrated in 888, and a similar establishment at Wilton in Wiltshire. Nothing remains to be seen at Altheney and Wilton, but at Shaftesbury the scant foundations of the Norman successor-church to the Saxon original have been excavated and left exposed to view. The great treasure at Shaftesbury is the lead casket which contained the bones of Edward the Martyr, canonised King of Wessex, who was murdered at Corfe Castle in 978. The relics of St Edward have, since their discovery in 1931, been kept in various places, and the matter of their final resting place is still being disputed more than 1000 years after the untimely demise of their owner.

The early Saxon houses were based on the Rule of St Benedict as elaborated in the sixth century; but monastic practice lapsed over the centuries and was almost extinguished as a result of the Viking raids in the ninth century, so that the revival of the abbeys in the second half of the tenth century, and especially during the reign of Edgar (957–75), involved the refounding of houses which had been abandoned. Much of the monastic renaissance was due to the efforts of a Somerset monk named Dunstan who went on to achieve great things as Archbishop of Canterbury. His most famous accomplishment was the revival of Glastonbury Abbey following his appointment as its abbot in 943, but he also brought back the monks to Bath, Cerne, Malmesbury and Sherborne. St Dunstan was in attendance at Bath on 11 May 973 when Edgar was crowned

King of England and a coronation service was used which still forms the basis of the present one. Edgar founded the great Benedictine Tavistock Abbey in 981, which, in spite of its destruction by the Danes in 997, achieved even greater renown thereafter. It was Edgar's *Regularis Concordia* of 970 that defined English monastic practice as essentially a liturgical observance providing the path to salvation.

By the eve of the Norman Conquest England already possessed about fifty monasteries and a dozen nunneries, but these figures were eventually to be left far behind by the zealous and energetic Normans. The first act of William the Conqueror after defeating Harold at Hastings in 1066 was to found Battle Abbey, but this was more a symbolic gesture of thanks for victory than a sign of a religious mission. In fact, the Norman prelates showed an initial hesitance to set up monastic houses in England; and when they did so, it was usually with an eye to gathering further revenues for the enrichment of abbeys at home. Monks had to be enticed away from the great houses of France, since many were reluctant to settle in what was regarded as a barbarous country. Encouraged, however, by grants of land and the support of the new Norman barons of England, anxious to redeem their souls by an act of piety, monastic colonisation gathered momentum in the closing years of the eleventh century. Cluniac foundations, with their strict insistence on liturgy and ceremony, were particularly popular at the outset, for example at Montacute Priory of 1102; but with the quest for higher ideals of monastic purity in the twelfth century a bracing wind of reform was to blow over from France, bringing more foundations, new orders and bigger buildings. Diffidence gave way to an insatiable appetite for land by the abbeys and priories to the extent that William of Malmesbury (1090–1143) was to complain that 'the newcomers devour the riches and entrails of England, and there is no hope of the misery coming to an end'.

The most impressive remains of the first phase of Norman abbeys in the characteristic round-arched style are now limited to a few examples in the West Country, due to subsequent rebuildings. The marvellous west door of St Germans Priory in Cornwall, although much eroded by the elements, is still a powerful display of typical Norman artistry with vigorous lines of zigzag incised into the portal. A minor essay in the style is preserved in the ruins of Torre Abbey in Torquay, the wealthiest English house of the Premonstratensian canons, where the entrance to the chapter houses still stands. Bristol Cathedral, as already noted in the previous chapter, contains some splendid Norman features of the former abbey of the Augustinian order.

William of Malmesbury would have witnessed much of the construction of the splendid Romanesque or Norman church of Malmesbury Abbey, although not its completion which was not achieved until 1180. What remains, albeit in mutilated form, is the great west front with its graceful interlaced arcading; and inside there are the massive round piers bearing the slightly pointed arches of the six bays of the truncated nave. However, the chief glory at Malmesbury Abbey is the south porch which is so full of Biblical carvings that it could be likened to a picture book in stone, designed for instruction as well as decoration. The seven round arches, recessed within one another, create the illusion of a tunnel leading straight into the church; but it is essential to stop within the porch and to look up above the inner door to view a carving of Christ in Majesty, and in *tympana* to left and right facing one another across the porch are portrayals of the Apostles with an angel hovering over them. The grace, dignity and gentleness of touch of these sculptures in full relief are in stark contrast to the crude vigour normally associated with the Normans, and it is supposed that they are the work of Saxon craftsmen. Possibly the Norman builders only permitted this expression of native

The west door of St Germans, Cornwall, is a masterpiece of strong Norman design.

talent in a position where it would not be too conspicuous. Be that as it may, the shelter of the porch has had the effect of preserving these unique pieces of Saxon art for posterity.

One of the greatest contributions to the monastic movement of the twelfth century was provided by a native of Somerset, Stephen Harding, who entered the monastery at Sherborne. His search for a more exalted and idealistic form of monasticism took him to France where he became the main founding father of a new order at Cîteaux in Burgundy. Harding's *Carta Caritatis* of 1119 established the Rule of the Cistercians, an order that was to exert tremendous influence throughout Europe. William of Malmesbury wrote of Stephen Harding: 'it redounds to the glory of England to have produced the distinguished man who was the author and promoter of that rule.' Notable Cistercian foundations in the West Country were at Bindon and Forde in Dorset, Buckfast, Buckland and Dunkeswell in Devon and Cleeve in Somerset. The Cistercian ideal of self-reliance and an austere lifestyle led them to remote places, where they set about making a living from the land. Although the Cistercians eschewed the

The great barn at Bradford-on-Avon, Wiltshire, was built by a tenant of the Abbess of Shaftesbury for the receipt of tithes from his subtenants.

A picturesque view (left) of Milton Abbey, Dorset. This grandiose building project was never completed; only the choir and transepts were built.

The cloisters of Lacock Abbey have been miraculously preserved within the rebuilt house.

acquisition of rent-producing properties, in contrast to the practice of the well-endowed Benedictine houses, they became extremely wealthy as a result of their efficient farming, and they benefited more than any other order from the hugely rich rewards of the wool industry as it boomed in the fourteenth and fifteenth centuries.

The Carthusians also left their mark on the West Country. It was at Witham in Somerset that the first English establishment of the Charterhouse order was founded in 1178–9. What survives here is the church of the *conversi* or lay brothers, who supplied the manual labour necessary for the upkeep of the monks, who spent their time essentially within their 'cells' – actually two-room dwellings with small gardens. The second Carthusian foundation in England was also in Somerset, at Hinton. Hinton's church has disappeared along with the cells of the monks, but there remains the remarkable structure of the thirteenth-century chapter house with the library above it and a fine dovecote below the roof. This attractive building is on private land but it can be viewed from the roadside. Other parts of the monastic complex have been absorbed by later residential developments.

The Gilbertine order, a mixed community of nuns and canons, was named after its creator Gilbert, who refounded the house at Amesbury in Wiltshire in 1177 and who is chiefly remembered for the eccentricity of his teaching methods. These included a lecture to the nuns on chastity which Gilbert delivered, according to Gerald of Wales, completely naked and 'hairy, emaciated, scabrous and wild'. A more conventional nunnery was that at Lacock founded by Ela, Countess of Salisbury in 1229 for Augustinian canonesses. This became a favourite refuge for daughters of aristocratic families who felt called to the religious life. The style of this wealthy and well-connected establishment can still be savoured in the ornate quality of the finely preserved cloisters. However, the undisputed leader among the nunneries of England as a whole was the great house of the Benedictines at Shaftesbury founded by Alfred the Great. Royal patronage and pilgrimage traffic to the relics of St Edward, king and martyr, assured the continuing fortunes of Shaftesbury Abbey to the extent that it was mischievously said that 'if the Abbess of Shafton (Shaftesbury) were to wed the Abbot of Glaston (Glastonbury) their heir would own more land than the King'. By the nature of things the matter could not be put to the test, but the wealth of both houses was of generous proportions.

At the time of the Dissolution it was reported of Glastonbury that the abbey was 'the goodliest house of that sort that ever we have seen . . . a house mete for the kinges majesty and for no man else . . . greate, goodly and so princely that as we have not seen the lyke . . .' The Benedictines of Glastonbury derived their revenues not only from a clever exploitation of King Arthur's relics, which some have denounced as a dishonest fabrication, to promote the lucrative pilgrimage business; they were also active improvers of their vast estates and pioneered the early schemes to drain the Somerset Levels to make the area suitable for agriculture. The scant remains of the once mighty Glastonbury Abbey still manage to convey a sense of the majesty of the building as it arose once more in the thirteenth century following the fire of 1184. The abbey church alone was 550 ft long. As a testimonial to the princely state of the Abbot of Glastonbury there can be nothing more evocative than the unique kitchen building, a magnificent square structure with an octagonal roof under an imposing stone lantern. This luxurious kitchen was exclusively devoted to catering for the needs of the Abbot's household; the community had a quite separate arrangement.

Other tangible relics of the wealth of monasteries are the great barns built expressly to receive the tithe or, in many cases, the agricultural produce grown by the abbey itself. Glastonbury's barn now houses the Somerset Rural Life Museum. Other notable survivals include the 'Spanish Barn' at Torre Abbey, so called because it housed prisoners from the Armada in 1588; and the barn at Buckland Abbey also bears signs of warlike preoccupation with its medieval fortified wall with slit-openings erected as a precaution against attacks from across the Channel. The barn at Abbotsbury in Dorset is now used for storing thatch, whereas the surviving half of the barn at Cerne Abbas in the same county has been converted into a private dwelling. Most splendid of all is the great barn at Bradford-on-Avon, 168 ft in length and made of smoothly cut oolitic limestone with the sturdy buttresses characteristic of this class of building. The excellent preservation of these barns is due to their practical, secular function which allowed them to be exempted from the general destruction of the Dissolution. Indeed, there was a specific instruction to the King's commissioners to 'pull down to

The Cistercian foundation of Cleeve Abbey in Somerset has retained a remarkable range of domestic quarters and a splendid gatehouse which were rebuilt shortly before the Dissolution.

The Abbot's Kitchen at Glastonbury Abbey was an example of monastic indulgence.

the ground all the walls of the churches, steeples, cloisters, fraters, dorters, chapter-houses, with all other houses, saving them that be necessary for a farmer'.

The horrors of the Dissolution could not have been even remotely anticipated as the abbeys and priories rose to new magnificence in the second half of the fourteenth century following the ravages of the Black Death in 1348. However, building ambitions often exceeded resources, and even the wealthiest, such as Glastonbury and Shaftesbury, would fall into debt. At Milton Abbey in Dorset an acute shortage of funds led to a curtailment of work on the abbey church with only the choir, crossing and transepts completed after the fire of 1309. The central tower was not erected until the second half of the fifteenth century, and the nave itself was never built.

Although religious fervour and enthusiasm for the monastic ideal were to start falling off in the fifteenth century, there was no letting up with building activity, but the accent was less on churches than on improving the comfort and style of the ancillary buildings. There was a particular trend towards even greater luxury and privacy for the prelates, as evidenced by the Abbot's House at Muchelney with its wall paintings, linenfold panelling, coffered oak ceiling, wagon roof and finely carved Renaissance-style stone fireplace. At Cerne Abbas the abbot's lodging was provided with its own elaborate gatehouse. The fifteenth-century gatehouse at Montacute Priory is an exquisite composition of oriel windows, battlements and octagonal turrets. At Cleeve Abbey the monks acquired a splendid new frater in the fifteenth-century with one of the finest timber roofs in the West Country, and the gatehouse was to be remodelled in the sixteenth century and embellished with a Latin motto which has been translated as: 'Gate be open, shut to no honest person', proclaiming the ancient tradition of monastic hospitality.

Church building was not entirely neglected during this Indian summer of the monasteries in England, for there are examples of ambitious late medieval building projects at Bath and Sherborne. The splendour of the fan-vaulting at these abbeys, and especially at Sherborne, is one of the most glorious achievements of the entire monastic era. The building at Sherborne was interrupted in 1437 as a result of a long-running dispute between the monks and the townsfolk over access to the font of the abbey church. An irate citizen of Sherborne fired a flaming arrow into the thatch which provided temporary cover for the newly commenced choir vault. The ensuing fire has left an indelible souvenir in the reddened patch of masonry which is still clearly visible. The monks won that particular argument, and one imagines that work proceeded without further incident once tempers had cooled to complete a fan-vaulted nave by the beginning of the sixteenth century to rival anything that can be seen elsewhere in England. Sherborne's fan-vaulting has a style of its own that was imitated elsewhere in the region, notably at Wells Cathedral and at Milton Abbey. The townsfolk of Sherborne were eventually to have the last laugh in their epic argument with the monks, for they acquired the wondrous abbey church in mint condition after the Dissolution, and it still serves the town as one of the most magnificent parish churches in all England.

The conspicuous wealth of the monasteries, especially those of the Benedictines, was countered to a certain extent by the austere lifestyle of the mendicant orders of the Carmelites, Dominicans and Franciscans. These, the White, Black and Grey Friars respectively, concentrated their efforts in the towns and cities and undertook many acts of charity which may be likened to urban relief programmes of our own age. Their churches aimed less at achieving the effect of magnificence than at providing convenient houses for preaching. Because of their typically urban location their sites have nearly all been built over in subsequent inner-city redevelopments. Of the friaries in large cities such as Exeter and Plymouth nothing has survived; but in Bristol the house of the Dominicans still stands in the very heart of the modern city and is now known as the Quaker Friars.

By the sixteenth century, however, not even the dedication of the friars was enough to redeem the overall picture of declining standards, lax practices and rampant corruption as reported back to Henry VIII and his chief henchman Thomas Cromwell. The reports were obviously heavily biased, aiming as they did to give some moral pretext to the real purpose of the Dissolution, which was nothing less than the expropriation of all monastic property. The wording of the Act of Suppression of 1536, which dissolved the abbeys and priories worth less than £200 a year, stated unequivocally in its preamble: 'Forasmuch

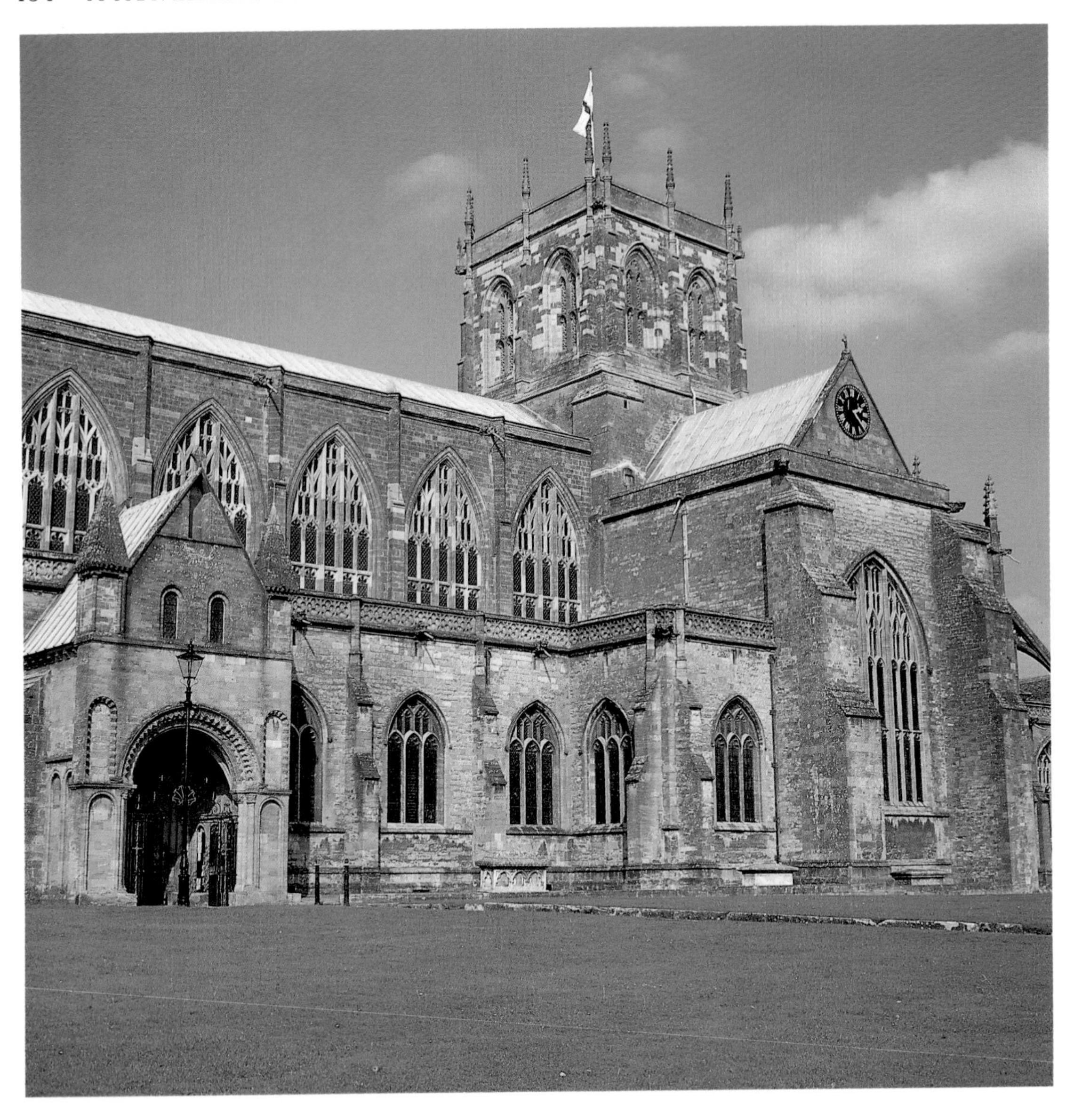

The glorious honey-coloured limestone from Ham Hill gives Sherborne Abbey in Dorset its characteristic warm glow, even under mild sunshine.

The principal glory of Sherborne Abbey's interior is the breathtaking fan vaulting of the nave which is flooded with light from the vast Perpendicular windows.

The west door of Buckfast Abbey, Devon, bears the imprint of twentieth-century Gothic style.

as manifest sin, vicious, carnal and abominable living, is daily used and committed against the little and small abbeys, priories and other religious houses'. There had always been instances of corruption and immorality, but now they were catalogued and emphasised out of all proportion. Dr Layton's report of 1535 from Bath during the preparatory phase of the Dissolution is fairly typical: 'we found the prior a right virtuose man and I suppose no better of his cote, a man simple and not of the greteste wit, his monkes worse than I have any founde yet both in bugerie and adulterie sum one of them having x women sum viii and the reste so fewer.' Such indictments of monastic malpractice helped to smooth the passage of the Act of Suppression which sounded the death knell for the smaller houses. The larger houses were picked off one by one using a variety of tactics which maintained the pretence of voluntary surrender. Where the co-operation of the prelates was not forthcoming, royal wrath and retribution was swift to descend. The most notorious case was the brutal execution of the elderly Abbot of Glastonbury. It was clinically related to Thomas Cromwell by Lord Russell on 16 November 1539 in the following terms:

> My lord, this shall be to ascertain you that on Thursday the 14th day of this present month the abbot of Glastonbury was arraigned, and the next day put to execution, with two other of his monks, for robbing of Glastonbury church, on Tor Hill, next unto the town of Glastonbury, the said abbot's body being divided into four parts, and the head stricken off; whereof one quarter standeth at Wells, another at Bath, and at Ilchester and Bridgwater the rest, and his head upon the abbey gate at Glastonbury . . .

The abbot's crime had been an attempt to conceal some of the abbey's plate from the King's commissioners.

By 1540 the Dissolution was completed. In practical terms it meant that the abbeys and priories were first relieved of their portable treasures, such as the plate which the Abbot of Glastonbury so unwisely tried to hide; then the valuable lead was stripped from the roofs and melted down, often the exquisitely carved woodwork of the churches being used to fuel the fire. In this way the monasteries were made immediately uninhabitable, and demolition was also carried out 'for fear the birds should build therein again'. Books and manuscripts were disposed of as so much waste paper or used as cleaning materials.

In spite of the overall destruction the West Country has conserved some evocative relics of a rich monastic heritage. The Augustinian abbey at Bristol was spared to serve in its new capacity as Bristol Cathedral. The churches of other abbeys such as Malmesbury, Milton, Sherborne and Dunster were retained for parochial use. Others were sold off to the new generation of wealthy Tudor gentry so that parts of the monastic buildings were incorporated into country houses as occurred at Forde, Lacock and Milton. At Buckland the house of Sir Richard Grenville was actually fashioned out of the church itself, and one runs across several architectural features such as pointed arches and window tracery in the most unexpected places. The Benedictine priory at St Michael's Mount served as a castle before being converted into a comfortable home. Elsewhere the abbeys disappeared entirely under new residences as at Hartland, Longleat and Wilton. There is the occasional odd survival such as the lavatorium at Sherborne which found a new function as a market cross. Among the most extensive ruins are the abbeys of Cleeve, Glastonbury and Muchelney in Somerset, but some of the grandest such as Tavistock have been badly dismembered over the years.

Thus Henry VIII achieved the extinction of the monastic life in England. In the West Country the desolation has been relieved by two notable revivals. Downside Abbey in Somerset was re-established from France at its present location in 1814, and the imposing Neo-Gothic church was constructed between 1870–1938. A more exciting development occurred in 1907 at Buckfast in Devon when a community of Benedictine monks began the reconstruction of the monastery on the exact foundations of the original Cistercian house which had lain abandoned since the Dissolution. The rebuilding of the church and cloister was accomplished in the best monastic tradition by the efforts of the monks themselves, although only one, Brother Peter, had any experience as a mason. The abbey church was formally completed with the final capping stone in 1937. By such endeavours has monasticism contrived to regain a foothold in the region.

The gatehouse of Exeter's Rougemont Castle goes back to early Norman times.

Forts and Castles

The need to build strongholds goes back in the West Country, as elsewhere in Britain, to the era of the Neolithic when the accent was firmly on communal defence with no obvious strategic purpose. Tribal security also appears as the overriding motive behind the great hillforts of the Iron Age, designed for the shelter of the local populace in those turbulent times. It was the Romans who introduced to the region the notion of military forts as outposts of a deliberate policy of conquest, but with the collapse of Roman rule at the beginning of the fifth century there was no coherent defence plan on the part of the Britons beyond the throwing up of enormously long earthworks such as the Wansdyke which would have been impossible to man effectively. The basic response to the westward advance of the Saxons was to re-occupy the hillforts, which had lain deserted for about 400 years, and to improvise some sort of refuge. The most impressive example of this type was excavated at South Cadbury in Somerset at the end of the 1960s. The archaeological remains showed that these were no hasty defences but a stoutly built rampart of stone interlaced with timber to support a wooden fighting platform. Although following the entire 1200-yd perimeter of the Iron Age earthwork, this rampart amounted to a virtually new fortification of the site. The dating of this work and of the generously proportioned (63 by 34 ft) hall within to around the beginning of the sixth century has given solid archaeological support to South Cadbury's legendary claim as King Arthur's Camelot.

Some three hundred years later it was the turn of the Saxons in the ninth century to play the role of defenders of the homeland against foreign aggressors, this time the Danes. Once again the West Country witnessed a decisive clash of arms as the destiny of the whole of England was contested. It was during the winter of early 878 that the Danes broke the undertakings given to Alfred at Wareham and Exeter and seized Chippenham from the West Saxons. Over the coming months the Danish king Guthrum ravaged Wiltshire, Hampshire and Dorset. Alfred was forced to take refuge in the swamps of the Somerset Levels at a place called Athelney; and it was only thanks to the heroic support of the men of Somerset that he was able to rally a force sufficiently strong to strike back victoriously at the Danes at the battle of Eddington in Wiltshire. Alfred's redoubt at Athelney, described as 'something of a fort', was probably a modest construction compared to the 'Arthurian' stronghold at South Cadbury, consisting of a ditched and palisaded stockade. Sadly, no trace has been discovered of this most significant structure, where during the spring of 878 the fate of the entire English people hung in the balance. Without the resistance of Somerset the way would have been open for the Danes into the very heart of the West Country.

It is one of those ironies of history that the two great folk heroes, Arthur the Celt and Alfred the Saxon, would have been enemies in the fifth and sixth centuries. However, by the time of the Danish invasions of the ninth century, Celt and Saxon had common cause, living in peaceful co-existence throughout most of the region, albeit with a concentration of Cornish Celts west of the Tamar holding outsiders at bay. The sense of shared destiny between the two main ethnic groups occupying the West Country was doubtless strengthened by the events of the late eleventh century when the alien civilisation of the Norman conquerors surged westward after the victory at Hastings in 1066.

On the face of it the West Saxons were to a certain extent prepared for invasion as a result of Alfred's creation of the 'burhs' or fortified towns, which are still in evidence at places such as Wareham in Dorset and Lydford in Devon. But these earthworks were no challenge to the armies of William the Conqueror and no match for the new generation of Norman castles which mushroomed after the Conquest, studding the English landscape like so many nails in the Anglo-Saxon coffin. It can be argued that Hastings did not really signify the defeat of the English, and that this victory was more akin to a kicking in of the front door. What followed, however, was the remorseless and emphatic crushing of English resistance throughout the land, achieved largely by the building of a host of castles.

Opposition in the west was exceptionally strong, meriting more than a historical footnote as the Western Rebellions. This bitter resistance occasioned William I to make a personal visit to Exeter in 1068, and it was the Conqueror himself who selected the site for the powerful Rougemont Castle, in a corner of the city where an entire neighbourhood was razed to the ground for the purpose. The main survival at Rougemont, one of the earliest of Norman castles in England, is the mighty but elegant gatehouse. A sign of its early date has been detected in the characteristic Saxon workmanship of the triangular-headed windows, indicating the employment of masons schooled in the old skills. But the essential identity of Rougemont Castle was resolutely Norman rather than anything remotely pre-Conquest.

The first generation of Norman castles were often no more than 'motte and bailey' types where the tower or keep on the 'motte' or mound was made of timber and the surrounding wall of the 'bailey' or enclosure was a palisade of tree trunks. Most of these wooden structures were soon replaced by castles of stone, as at Okehampton in Devon, slightly removed from the centre of today's town, and at Launceston in Cornwall which still dominates the town from its lofty motte. Several earthworks have survived without their castles, such as Castle Neroche in Somerset, thought to have been built as a temporary base during the Western Rebellion of 1067–9. Mounds without castles may be seen also at Dunster in the grounds of the present castle, at Barnstaple in the heart of the modern town, and at Marlborough within the confines of the College. At Montacute there was once a Norman castle on the original *mons acutus* or steep hill which gave the place its name. This was a particularly symbolic site for the English due to the discovery earlier in the eleventh century of a supposed fragment of the Holy Cross. The construction of a Norman castle on this spot was perceived as a highly offensive and provocative act. The castle was actually besieged by the English in 1069, but the uprising was put down with savage ferocity.

Cornwall possesses some outstanding Norman castles of the shell-keep variety such as Restormel, whose fortunes rose along with those of the once important town of Lostwithiel, and Trematon. The latter, set in peaceful farmland, now encloses a private residence and can only be viewed from the outside, whereas the full splendour of Restormel can still be savoured. The castle was acquired by Richard, Earl of Cornwall, shortly before his death in 1272, and it was probably his son Edmund who was responsible for the improvements made to the accommodation within the shell-keep, making this a sophisticated circular home set around a central courtyard. The shell-keep at Totnes in Devon was also improved early in the fourteenth century. Like the castle at Launceston, it really perches high above the town with the obvious intent to overawe the locals.

The most spectacular of the Norman

Restormel Castle, Cornwall, is a perfect specimen of the shell-keep type of fortification.

castles in the West Country is also one of the most ruinous, its devastated masonry still standing guard over a gap in the Purbeck Hills. Corfe Castle, whose name actually means 'gap', was in its original form one of the first sites to be fortified by the Normans, beginning life during the reign of William I. Its strategic location gave Corfe tremendous importance right into the seventeenth century when the Civil War reduced it to its present ruin. The golden age at Corfe occurred during the thirteenth century, especially in the reign of King John (1199–1216), when it was in active service in its capacities as royal residence, treasury and prison. To this period belongs the 'Gloriette', a residential range containing the King's Hall and Presence Chamber. The 'Gloriette' is noted for the excellence of its masonry; and the austere pointed arch of the main doorway into the hall is worthy of any cathedral or abbey in the Early English manner. Before its destruction by the Parliamentarian sappers in 1646 as retribution for its previous resistance under the spirited leadership of Lady Bankes, Corfe had been described as 'a very fayre castell', but today it looks as though its towers and concentric ramparts have been knocked about by a wilful giant or shattered by a mighty earthquake.

The onus of Norman castle-building fell heavily on the shoulders of the local populace. Especially during the 'anarchy' of the twelfth century before Henry II (1154–89) tamed the ambitions of his barons and restored the authority of the Crown, it must have been a harrowing time for the natives of England. *The Anglo-Saxon Chronicle* gave bitter expression to the grievances of the common people in a much-quoted passage from the year 1137:

> For every great man built him castles and held them against the King; and they filled the whole land with these castles. They

Corfe Castle's mass of tumbledown masonry still maintains a menacing presence guarding a strategic cap in Dorset's Purbeck Hills (left). *The devastation of Corfe Castle during the Civil War by the Parliamentarians is well attested by this gatehouse* (above) *which was literally rent asunder by the sappers.*

The ruins of Bishop Roger's castle at Old Sarum in Wiltshire.

> sorely burdened the unhappy people of the country with forced labour on the castles; and when the castles were built, they filled them with devils and wicked men.

Barons were not the only builders of castles. Roger, Bishop of Salisbury – before he fell from grace – was the most powerful man in the realm after Henry I himself, whom he served as Chancellor and subsequently Justiciar. Bishop Roger built himself a magnificent courtyard residence at Old Sarum within the Norman castle, and another at Sherborne. The ruinous remains at Sherborne, another victim of the Civil War, still manage to convey a sense of the quasi-regal state to which a church magnate might aspire in the first half of the twelfth century. The castellar effect given by the ditch, towers and walls was mainly for show since this was more of a princely residence than a serious fortification. Ralph of Shrewsbury, Bishop of Bath and Wells (1329–63), who created the picturesque moat and curtain wall around the Bishop's Palace at Wells, may have been spurred on by a real concern for his own personal safety. The fourteenth century was indeed marked by outbreaks of violent anti-clericalism, such as the murder of the

Bishop of Exeter in London in 1326 by an angry mob. The moated fortifications at Wells have a particular charm, for they can be viewed across open fields which provide an untrammelled vista of the curtain wall with the Bishop's Palace and the Cathedral rising proudly beyond.

With the waning of the Middle Ages the defensive role of castles gave way to a more symbolic show of rank and prestige. At Nunney in Somerset Sir John de la Mare had built for himself the most castellar of castles in a late fourteenth century style borrowed directly from the current fashions of France. Set on low-lying ground in the midst of its host village, the lofty towers linked by a machicolated fighting gallery are strangely impressive but lack the authority proper to a castle, so that the general effect of Nunney is of prettiness rather than power. Not surprisingly, the castle failed to resist the cannon of Cromwell's men during the Civil War due to its exposed position close to rising ground. Not far away at Farleigh, Sir Thomas de Hungerford set about the refortification of his manor house. Walter Lord Hungerford, his son and heir, Member of Parliament and veteran of the Battle of Agincourt, continued the work commenced by his father,

Norman architecture in evidence at Sherborne Old Castle in Dorset.

The square keep of Lydford Castle in Devon was built in the twelfth century to hold any transgressors of the extremely harsh forest and stannary statutes.

The proud remains of Launceston Castle, Cornwall, (right) *still loom large and imposing atop the lofty Norman motte.*

Nunney Castle, Somerset, is a poetic evocation of a French fourteenth-century chateau.

adding a barbican and an outer bailey which necessitated the enclosure of the parish church. Without further ado this became the private chapel to the castle and a repository for Hungerford grave monuments. The parish church was entirely rebuilt away from the castle of Farleigh Hungerford, as it is now known.

At Berry Pomeroy in Devon and Old Wardour in Wiltshire there is the enjoyable spectacle of Renaissance ideas entering the very fabric of medieval castles with the most pleasing results. Berry Pomeroy has been owned by only two families since the Conquest. From 1066 to 1548 it was in the possession of the de Pomeroys who built the medieval part of the castle. The surviving parts of this work, datable to about 1300, consist of the south curtain and a section of the west curtain together with a splendid twin-towered gatehouse where the two walls meet. Beyond this imposing entrance rises the Tudor mansion built inside the castle by the descendants of Edward Seymour, Lord Protector of Somerset, who acquired Berry Pomeroy in 1548. This purely residential three-storey block with its regular and generous fenestration strikes a thoroughly modern note within its medieval context. Unfortunately, this fine new accommodation was not properly completed when the Civil War caused work to be suspended, and the Seymours abandoned the place for good in 1688. After centuries of ivy-covered obscurity Berry Pomeroy is currently under the scaffolding of English Heritage and promises to re-emerge as one of the most fascinating of castles, to rival Old Wardour with which it has much in common.

Old Wardour was built at the very end of the fourteenth century following a licence to crenellate granted to the 5th Lord Lovel in 1393. The outline of the castle is lucidity itself, a regular hexagon with twin towers along one side and built around a central courtyard. Like Sir John de la Mare's fantasy at Nunney, Lord Lovel's conception at Old Wardour owed much to the sophisticated designs of France. When the castle was acquired in 1570 by Sir Matthew Arundell, the new owner commissioned a subtle transformation of the property from the leading architect of the day, Robert Smythson, best known for his work on Longleat and other great country houses of Elizabethan England. This involved the insertion of much larger mullioned windows in place of their narrower predecessors and the replacement of the medieval portcullis by a columned entrance bearing the heraldic device of the family. Inside the courtyard, the feel of Old Wardour is still decidedly medieval, but there are some enchanting Renaissance flourishes as well, most notably the round-arched portico with neatly fluted Classical columns which frame the staircase leading up to the hall on the first floor.

Even as more peaceful times at home were rendering obsolete the embattled strongholds of the Middle Ages, so the threat of invasion from Europe brought into being a new class of fortification. Fear of attack by the French led the citizens of Dartmouth to fortify their harbour entrance as early as the fourteenth century, and in the fifteenth a chain was stretched across the harbour mouth with the aid of a royal grant of £30 in 1462. Work on the present Dartmouth Castle began in 1481 and continued during the reign of Henry VII (1485–1509). This was the first castle in England to be designed principally for artillery but it was still partly medieval in concept with towers more for show than military purpose. In 1509–10 the way ahead was shown, again at Dartmouth, by Bayard's Cove, a small circular artillery fort with eleven gun ports, but this was soon to be superseded both in size and sophistication by the coastal defences of the reign of Henry VIII (1509–47).

Following Henry VIII's break with Rome and the establishment of the Church of England under the patronage of the monarch, fears were running high of a combined attack by the great Catholic powers of Europe. The entire southern coast of Britain appeared extremely vulnerable to invasion, so Henry VIII lost no time in building a string of forts along the coast which represented a revolution in the castellar architecture of the day. Designed uniquely for artillery and with no regard to royal or baronial pretensions, these squat, geometric buildings relied entirely on the latest scientific theories of effective lines of fire for their design. Circular towers provided an all-round view, and the internal accommodation, intended only for a garrison, was completely subjugated to the external shape of the forts. Work began in the south-east where the danger from across the Channel was felt to be most acute, and then rapidly spread westwards, with Portland Castle being completed by 1540. The funds for this emergency building programme came from the capital raised by the Dissolution of the Monasteries.

The courtyard of Old Wardour Castle, Wiltshire, shows the traces of a sixteenth-century modernisation with its Renaissance-style arch framing the medieval stairway.

Compton Castle, Devon, was refortified in the sixteenth century to deter raiding parties from across the Channel. The castle has undergone extensive repairs earlier this century.

Portland Castle, Dorset, was one of several sixteenth-century coastal artillery forts.

By 1545 work was finished on a pair of forts facing one another across the Fal estuary in Cornwall. St Mawes and Pendennis, both excellently conserved, are superb examples of the current state of the art of fortification in the mid-sixteenth century. Only in their immediate physical setting is there a marked contrast between them. This was well described by Richard Carew in his *Survey of Cornwall* of 1603: 'St Mawes lies lower and better to annoy shipping, but Pendennis standeth higher and stronger to defend itself.' Apart from that essential difference, the forts are but variations on the single theme of circular defence. Pendennis is completely circular but for its projecting gatehouse, while at St Mawes the central round tower is surrounded by a trefoil of circular outworks which give an outline like an ace of clubs. Both bear the royal coat of arms above the entrance, but St Mawes is the more embellished of the two and displays a number of Latin inscriptions in praise of Henry VIII, such as that along the string course over the entrance which reads *Semper honos Henrice tuus laudesque manebunt* or 'Henry, thy honour and praises will remain for ever'. However, as Carew had suggested, the low-lying location of St Mawes made it extremely vulnerable on the landward side, and during the Civil War it capitulated to the Parliamentarians in 1646 after only a brief parley, whereas Pendennis held out for five months in the same year in one of the most heroically fought sieges, and was the last Royalist stronghold but one to fall.

In fact, the Civil War of the seventeenth century provided a last opportunity for many castles to play their original defensive role, and the destruction that one sees at places like Corfe Castle and Old Wardour is almost entirely due to the conflict of those years. With Royalists and Parliamentarians alike making use of the many existing strongholds, there was little need for new defensive buildings. It is thus quite a rarity to find within the confines of an island as small as Tresco both a King Charles's Castle and a Cromwell's Castle. The former consists actually of an angular defence constructed around a building of mid-sixteenth century date displaying the linear artillery structures which took over from the round shapes of St Mawes and Pendennis. The most impressive example in the West Country of the new angular style of fortification is the Royal Citadel at Plymouth of 1666–71. By that time the genuine castle of the Middle Ages had already been defunct for about two centuries. However, no sooner had the castle died as a reality than castle nostalgia emerged to carry forward the idea of the thing into the present. The movement may be seen already in the early seventeenth century at Lulworth Castle in Dorset, but this – along with the other mock castles through the ages – belongs more properly to the history of the English house. Even the genuine article, as happened to Old Wardour, could find itself in the eighteenth century reduced to a supporting role as an antiquarian object in a landscape of the Picturesque, a quaint 'Gothick' ruin.

St Mawes Castle, Cornwall, bears the hallmark of royal patronage on its imposing entrance.

Oldway, Paignton, brought the grandeur of Versailles to south Devon in the Edwardian era.

From Manor House to Stately Home

The ground in front of the Kings of Wessex School in Cheddar is riddled with concrete studs marking the post-holes of a Saxon palace complex dating back to the tenth and eleventh centuries, and referred to in documents of the day as '*villa celebris, palatium regis*'. The confusing proliferation of post-holes results from a series of rebuildings, but the main element of this rural palace was always the long hall in which the king would hold his court, meals would be taken, festivities celebrated, and which at the end of the day would serve further as a communal bedchamber. The long hall was thus the very heart and *raison d'être* of the establishment. When men of lesser rank built homes of their own in the centuries that followed, it was still the hall which dominated the planning of the accommodation. The switch from the timber of the Saxons to the stone of the Normans was a great leap forwards in building technology, but the creation of a worthy and noble hall remained the basic objective of the builders. Indeed, the hall continued to be a major feature of stately residences, albeit in varying guises, right into the twentieth century.

The earliest survival of a manorial hall in the West Country, though under a new roof, is the mid-twelfth-century north wing of Horton Court in Avon. At Clevedon Court in the same county, and within hailing distance of the M5 motorway, the fourteenth century hall has survived despite the later insertion of an intermediate floor, a common practice as may be seen at Sheldon Manor in Wiltshire and elsewhere, which had the dual advantage of providing additional living space and snugger, more intimate rooms. One of the best places to experience the authentic feel of a modest, medieval hall is Fiddleford Mill House in Dorset, probably built for William Latimer, Sheriff of Somerset and Dorset, during the last quarter of the fourteenth century. Half of the hall and the solar wing are intact, displaying the full glory of their open timber roofs with trusses constructed in the typical West Country fashion. At Dartington in Devon the fourteenth century hall, built by a half-brother of Richard III, was a roofless structure when taken in hand by its new owners in 1925, but it remains a precious relic of the Middle Ages under its new oak roof of hammerbeam type built in the traditional manner. Even lesser members of the country gentry contrived to make a fine display: the Old Post Office at Tintagel in Cornwall was not a quaint pixie cottage, as may be supposed from its delightfully sagging roof, but a modest manor with a central hall inside, open to the roof timbers.

During the course of the early Middle Ages the communal nature of the hall was already in decline due to the changing lifestyle of the lord and his lady who sought ever more privacy in the solar. By the end of the Middle Ages the hall was mainly used for the meals of the lord's retinue and on special festive occasions when it continued to play an important symbolic role. At Great Chalfield in Wiltshire, the hall is still the dominant feature of the house, but in addition to the solar at one end of the hall there is also at the other end a separate dining room for the family to take their meals in privacy. This is an excellent illustration of the trend described by Langland in *Piers Plowman* of the hall falling into disfavour:

> There the lord and lady liketh not to sit;
> Now have the rich a rule to eat by themselves
> In a privy parlour . . .

The privy parlour at Great Chalfield was

Athelhampton, Dorset, embodies the manorial style of the late Middle Ages.

certainly an innovation in its day; and a mural painting of Thomas Tropnell, the man who had it built between 1465–80, has been discovered behind the sixteenth-century oak panelling.

Another splendid late-medieval manor house is Athelhampton in Dorset, built around 1485 by Sir William Martyn, a businessman who became Lord Mayor of London in 1493. The battlemented house with its baronial hall is not only an example of the trappings of the Middle Ages living on into Tudor times but also of the growing trend of wealthy men in the City of London continuing a parallel role as country magnates. Of the same period is the manor at Cotehele in Cornwall, built by Sir Richard Edgcumbe in the rambling medieval style around internal courtyards. The 40-ft long hall, the work of his son Sir Piers Edgcumbe, is one of the noblest baronial productions of its day in the West Country. Constructed at the time when the full sun of the English Renaissance was dawning elsewhere in the land, it showed that Cornwall was still lagging behind and experiencing primitive conditions. The hall at Cotehele would certainly have witnessed the medieval squalor so graphically described by Erasmus as being still the norm in many noble English houses, whose floors were 'strewed with rushes, beneath which lies an ancient collection of beer, grease, fragments, bones, spittle, excrement of dogs and cats, and everything that is nasty'. It is necessary to call to mind the words of Erasmus when visiting the sanitised manorial halls in the care of English Heritage and the National Trust, in order to fill in some of the essential, albeit unsavoury details of the medieval scene.

The marvellous preservation of the original appearance of Cotehele is due to the fact that the Edgcumbe family made no alterations to the house beyond the building of the north-west tower in 1627. Instead of attempting to bring their old home up to date with a Renaissance façade or two, they created an entirely new family seat at Mount Edgcumbe on a lofty peninsula overlooking Plymouth Sound. This noble residence was the opposite of Cotehele in every respect. Commanding a majestic vista from its hilltop site, Mount Edgcumbe was outward-looking and full of light from its generous and regular rows of windows. Cotehele was quite literally hidden away, as its name, meaning 'wood in the estuary', suggests. Mount Edgcumbe, in further contrast to Cotehele and most other houses of

Cotehele, Cornwall, represents the final expression of medieval domesticity in the region.

Trerice, Cornwall, retains the huge window of the ancient Great Hall in a façade which aims otherwise to reflect the fashion of Renaissance symmetry.

Barrington Court, Somerset, a sixteenth-century house of imposing character, has the E-shape which was so popular in Elizabethan England.

its date in the middle of the sixteenth century, was conceived as a single entity without a central courtyard. The baronial presence was indicated by purely decorative battlements and circular towers at the corners which were replaced by the present octagonal ones in 1749. Sadly, the interior of Mount Edgcumbe was totally destroyed in 1941 by a stray incendiary bomb aimed at Devonport, but the house has been reconstructed within its burnt-out shell so that the exterior still conveys a faithful image of the openness and symmetry of its Renaissance-style elevations. The idea of the hall has not been completely discarded but merely transformed into a grand central vestibule which gives spatial cohesion to the house.

Mount Edgcumbe, in respect of its rational planning, represented an advance on other houses of the first half of the sixteenth century such as Barrington Court in Somerset where the appearance of symmetry is revealed on closer inspection to be less than perfect with varying numbers of gables on the different elevations. Internally too, Barrington Court is irregular, with the hall placed to one side according to ancient practice. Even at Longleat in Wiltshire, completed in its present form in the 1570s, and generally acclaimed as the greatest monument of Elizabethan architecture, the quest for absolute symmetry did not entirely succeed, although it requires a meticulous observer to note the slight variations of fenestration. These quirks were caused by the fact that Longleat is in reality not a complete child of the Renaissance but a comprehensive rebuilding around a medieval courtyard house, which in turn was created from an ancient Carthusian monastery. Turrets of the earlier building stick up in places from behind the parapets of the Renaissance façade. Nevertheless, Longleat is of more than regional significance as one of the great prodigy houses of the Elizabethan age, where the parade of majesty takes over as the dominating influence on the planning.

The sixteenth century is also notable for the charm and beauty of many, more modest productions. Cadhay in Devon, Lytes Cary and Brympton d'Evercy in Somerset, and Sandford Orcas in Dorset all display pleasing Renaissance features which speak of Tudor peace and security following the turbulence of the Wars of the Roses of the previous century. However, fortifications were needed exceptionally, as may be seen at Compton Castle in Devon where the main front of the house was completely fortified as a protection against French raiders. But the hallmark of the age was growing refinement reflected above all in the natural outward elegance of houses such as Trerice in Cornwall, whose fanciful east façade of around 1570 sports an attractive array of decorative scrolled gables. Playfulness is the major characteristic of Montacute in Somerset, built for Sir Edward Phelips, Speaker in the House of Commons and Master of the Rolls, from about 1590. Montacute has the essential Elizabethan quality of whimsical invention, so well shown by the two delightful pavilions set in opposite corners of the garden to the east of the house.

In Elizabethan and Jacobean houses the hall had to contend not only with the proliferation of private apartments but also with that splendid new feature of stately homes, a long gallery designed to contain the growing art collections of their cultivated owners. Significantly, the Great Hall at Montacute is a modest affair of only one storey in height, but the Long Gallery above runs the entire length of the house, some 172 ft in all. It is now used most appropriately for exhibiting a selection of Elizabethan paintings from the National Portrait Gallery. Possibly the most spectacular long gallery in the West Country is that at Lanhydrock House in Cornwall. The truly wonderful plaster barrel ceiling displays a dazzling array of scenes from the Old and New Testament. It was scarcely finished in 1642 at the outbreak of the Civil War, which also caused the suspension of work on the

Tuscan columns are the main feature of Godolphin House in Cornwall.

charming two-storeyed gatehouse; this pretty barbican was not completed until 1651. The hostilities also effectively ended the building of Godolphin House in Cornwall, but the impressive loggia of 1635 had been completed, forming a sturdy structure supported by Tuscan columns fashioned from the local granite.

The Civil War, generally speaking, also stands as a well-defined cultural divide marking the end of the exuberance of the Elizabethans and Jacobeans. However, at Wilton House in Wiltshire the dawning of the purer, Neoclassical style of architecture actually preceded the conflict of the 1640s. The influence of Inigo Jones has been detected in the south front of Wilton which was designed by Isaac de Caus and seen through to completion after a disastrous fire in 1647 by John Webb, the main

Sandford Orcas, Dorset, is a Classic among the smaller sixteenth-century houses of the gentry.

One of the garden pavilions at Montacute, Somerset, (right) *shows the pleasing Elizabethan playfulness which enlivens the architecture of the period.*

Tableau at Littlecote, Wiltshire, shows a scene in the life of the house during the Civil War.

upholder of Jones's Palladian ideals after the death of the master in 1652. The most striking part of the Jonesian legacy at Wilton are the two state rooms known on account of their exact proportions as the Single Cube and the Double Cube; these are rooms of extreme refinement and regal decoration. The Double Cube was used for the most lavish dinners and festivities; but that is about all it had in common with its historical ancestor, the great hall of centuries past. Here at Wilton we are confronted with a world far removed from the colourful and intimate conviviality of the Middle Ages with its attendant squalour. The rarefied atmosphere speaks more of devotion to noble ideas of abstract style than to anything so humdrum as domestic comfort. Wilton is closer in spirit to the princely courts of Europe than to anything of its own region.

The switch from Elizabethan to Classical can be observed at Brympton d'Evercy where the south front of about 1697 shows palatial aspirations with its noble composition of alternating triangular and segmental pediments above the windows. Antony House in Cornwall, rebuilt between 1710–

21 by Sir William Carew, is a wonderful example of its date of a sobre Classical façade held together visually by a neat pediment. The lack of ornamentation may be mainly due to the intractable qualities of the grey Pentewan stone, but that sort of reticence was considered entirely appropriate in the early years of the eighteenth century when austere Palladianism was ousting the livelier English Baroque as practised by Vanbrugh among others at grand houses such as Kings Weston in Bristol.

The earliest of the purely Palladian country houses, with its strict adherence to the rules, was the mansion built at Stourhead in Wiltshire in 1721–4 by the banker Henry Hoare. This astute gentleman was well abreast of the coming fashion and did not hesitate over the design of his new house but 'immediately bought Mr Campbell's books', as he himself declared with pride. Colen Campbell was one of the arch exponents of the Palladian revival of the 1720s, but the essential point of interest at Stourhead is not the architecture of the house, though still recognisable for what it is despite subsequent modifications, but the marvellous landscape created by Henry Hoare II from 1744. This Henry Hoare, the son and heir of the first, is distinguished from others of that name in the family by the epithet 'the Magnificent' as if in mock emulation of a Turkish Sultan. The title is indeed well deserved, for what Henry Hoare II achieved at Stourhead, the creation of a private paradise in a fantasy landscape, would have given supreme satisfaction to any Oriental potentate. In this setting of intense beauty Henry the Magnificent could withdraw from the cares of everyday life which included a career as a banker. Hoare's Bank, quite fittingly, made a tidy profit from huge loans advanced to the many noblemen who embarked at that time on costly and ambitious improvements to their estates.

At the heart of the Stourhead landscape is the vast artificial lake, which is used in the most enchanting manner to set off a succession of architectural delights such as the Temple of Flora, the Pantheon and the Temple of Apollo, designed by Henry Flitcroft. The Classical ambiance was completed by the Palladian Bridge, a noble structure which was borrowed directly from an engraving published in the English edition of Giacomo Leoni's *The Architecture of Palladio*. To these symbols of Classical antiquity was added a dose of mystery and romanticism by the Grotto, a domed subterranean chamber dimly lit from a circular opening overhead. A statue of a nymph reclined in sleep slumbers over a cascade fed by a natural spring. Opposite the exit from the Grotto is the River God's Cave, occupied by a powerful statue of the river god himself. This type of fantasy grotto was a recurrent feature of English gardens in the eighteenth century; and there is another wonderful example in the grounds of Goldney House in Bristol, created in 1739 by Thomas Goldney, the grandson of a Quaker grocer. The grotto at Goldney is less grandiose in conception than that at Stourhead, but its lavish and fanciful decoration with shells and stones is of exceptional artistry.

The inspiration at Stourhead was, however, not entirely Classical. Gothic elements, otherwise eschewed by the Palladians in serious works of architecture, were quite acceptable as follies in a park or garden. Thus we find at Stourhead two rather awkward structures known as the Convent and the Gothic Cottage posing rather self-consciously as medieval curiosities. Forming a distant visual reference point on the crest of a hill stands the vaguely medieval, 160-ft high Alfred's Tower, erected to mark the supposed spot where the Saxon king raised his standard against the Danes. There is even a genuine relic of medieval England at Stourhead in the shape of the reconstructed Bristol High Cross, removed as a traffic obstacle in 1733 and eventually acquired in 1765 by Henry Hoare II as an entertaining piece of garden architecture.

The Classical bridge at Wilton House, Wiltshire, reflects the fashion for artistic structures placed picturesquely in the landscape.

The lake at Stourhead, Wiltshire, (right) *is a fine product of eighteenth-century landscape theory.*

The rage for extravagant fantasy grottoes was another aspect of eighteenth-century landscape ideas. This fine example is in the grounds of Goldney House, Bristol.

The Classical remodelling of Saltram House, Devon, (left) follows the best taste of the age with its elegant niches occupied by statuary in the Roman manner.

parade their money and ancestral status, whether real or imagined.

To the Heathcoat-Amory family, who had built up in Tiverton the largest lace-making business in the world, the choice of the Gothic Revivalist William Burges to design their instant baronial home in 1869 was a natural one. Knightshayes Court was provided with an imposing Great Hall complete with screens passage and gallery. The medieval theme was continued throughout the house, and the vibrant colours of the Middle Ages, so beloved by Burges, were used to extravagant effect. Indeed, the effect was quite overpowering to later generations of Heathcoat-Amorys who Georgianised many of the interiors. The National Trust is now slowly returning Knightshayes Court to its original and garish Victorian splendour. There is a pleasing touch to be noted. The vista enjoyed by the house includes the factory chimney of the Heathcoat works in Tiverton; this is no medieval sham but an unadorned piece of industrial architecture. In spite of the baronial pretensions of his mansion Sir John Heathcoat-Amory was not ashamed to acknowledge in this way the source of his considerable fortune.

At Dunster Castle in Somerset and St Michael's Mount in Cornwall the architects were able to graft Victorian castellation on to existing ancient structures occupying dramatic sites; and at Lanhydrock House in Cornwall a disastrous fire in 1881 provided the opportunity for an extensive rebuilding in a Victorian pastiche of medieval architecture. At the very end of the nineteenth century the heir to the legacy of the W. H. Smith bookselling empire built himself near Moretonhampstead on the eastern flank of Dartmoor what has been described as a 'Tudor Castle', which contained a lofty, oak-panelled Great Hall with screen and minstrel gallery beneath a magnificent timber roof. The same fate that had happened to many of the genuine halls of the Middle Ages, befell this one completed in 1907: an intermediate floor was later inserted to make more space in its subsequent role as an hotel.

Without doubt the most spectacular of the baronial revivals in the West Country is Castle Drogo, also on the eastern flank of Dartmoor, which was designed by the renowned architect Lutyens for Julius Drew who had amassed a quick fortune as founder of the Home and Colonial Stores. Julius Drew took the baronial part very seriously and convinced himself that he was descended from the Drewes of Broadhembury near Honiton, and a genealogist produced a pedigree which showed descent from a Drogo or Dru, a Norman who had come over to England with the Conqueror himself. Castle Drogo, the new ancestral home of the Drews built between 1911–30, is one of the most medieval and modern of buildings at the same time. It offers a rare aesthetic experience, betraying the hand of a master architect. Castle Drogo stands at the end of a long and ancient tradition of English building.

The Gothic Revivalists did not have it all their own way, however, in the nineteenth century. The remodelling of Kingston Lacy in Dorset by Charles Barry from 1835–41 took up the Classical theme as it encased the Restoration period house of 1663–5 designed by Sir Roger Pratt for Sir Ralph Bankes, whose ancestral home of Corfe Castle had been rendered totally uninhabitable during the Civil War. This enforced move from the ancient castle was commemorated during the building of the new Kingston Lacy by a full-length bronze statue of Lady Bankes holding the key to Corfe Castle in one hand and a sword in the other. In honour of her courageous resistance the Parliamentarians allowed her to retain the key to Corfe Castle, and it still hangs on display at Kingston Lacy, as a token of genuine medieval ancestry.

Classical architecture made one last, but spectacular appearance in the West Country at the mansion now known as Oldway at Paignton in Devon. The first building had been completed in 1875 as a pleasure

A bronze statue of Lady Bankes at Kingston Lacy holds the key to Corfe Castle.

retreat for the sewing-machine magnate Isaac Merritt Singer; and it was his third son Mr Paris Eugene Singer who gave Oldway its present, florid Edwardian aspect in 1904–7. The grand manner of Versailles provided much of the inspiration. The ceiling above the great staircase was actually copied from the original at Versailles, the influential Mr Singer having obtained permission for scaffolding to be erected to permit his painter Lebrun a close up view of the seventeenth-century brushwork. The interior of Oldway, a veritable orgy of marble, brass and heroic paintings, now serves as offices for the local council. *Sic transit gloria mundi.*

The House-that-Moved in Exeter was the home of a merchant in Tudor times.

From Village to City

Images of the West Country are so bound up with idyllic country cottages nestling in peaceful hamlets that it might seem inappropriate to consider the region in terms of its urban tradition. The sheer weight of the physical evidence, however, requires us to view towns and cities such as Bath, Bristol, Exeter, Plymouth and Salisbury as well as smaller places such as Blandford Forum and Bradford-on-Avon not as provincial curiosities but as noteworthy and sometimes outstanding forms of the urban phenomenon. The truth remains, nevertheless, that scattered hamlets are still the dominant feature of large parts of the region, especially in Cornwall. Here in the far west of the old Celtic domains, nucleated villages on the Saxon model are the exception, and one such is at Blisland on the fringe of Bodmin Moor where the houses are grouped around a picturesque green, among them a fine Norman house which has been incorporated into a later medieval residence.

The origins of urban life in the West Country have Saxon rather than Roman roots, for town life gradually disintegrated after the withdrawal of the Romans and was virtually extinguished for several centuries. When life later returned to some of the abandoned Roman cities such as Dorchester and Exeter it had nothing in common with the previous settlements but for the retention of the walls as the foundation for new fortifications. The Saxons were not urban pioneers by inclination and only assumed that role in the ninth century when the Kingdom of Wessex was under attack by the Danes. It was Alfred the Great who instituted the planned fortified settlements, known as the 'burhs', as a way of protecting life, limb and property in times of trouble. Thus it was the need for an effective defence of the native communities which led to the resumption of urban life in the region, as represented by the burhs, some 1100 years ago.

Alfred's biographer Asser wrote of 'the cities and towns he (Alfred) restored, and the others he constructed where there had been none before'. William of Malmesbury, writing in the early twelfth century, records an inscription in the chapter house at Shaftesbury stating that 'Alfred made this town' in 880. In fact, Shaftesbury served for a while as Alfred's capital, the hilltop providing a natural defence which was ready-made, before Winchester became the seat of royal authority in Wessex. The Iron Age fortifications of Old Sarum in Wiltshire were re-used in Saxon times to create a burh of such importance that the Normans later regarded it as a suitable place for the episcopal see of Sherborne to be transferred thither. Cricklade, on the eastern frontier of Wessex, is typical of the smaller rectangular burhs founded by Alfred. Its earthen rampart was faced with a timber revetment and topped by a timber palisade. Another rectangular burh, and one of the best preserved, is at Wareham in Dorset. This is the most visually rewarding of the burhs for the town of Wareham still stands substantially within its Saxon ramparts, which have actually become more pronounced in recent years since they were reinforced in 1940 against tank assault. The grid pattern of Wareham's present street plan goes back to late Saxon times. The later stone wall, erected on the Saxon earthwork in the Middle Ages, was subsequently dismantled so that Wareham's Alfredian origins are clearly revealed.

The Norman occupiers of the West Country were initially more concerned with castles than the creation of towns. In several

The cruck method of construction is clearly visible at this house in Lacock, Wiltshire.

places, large areas of Saxon towns were cleared to make way for Norman castles as at Exeter where forty-eight houses were demolished; and the same occurred elsewhere, notably at Bridport, Dorchester, Shaftesbury and Wareham in Dorset and at Barnstaple, Lydford and Totnes in Devon. Other towns were to be moulded by the shape of the motte and bailey, as may be observed most clearly at Devizes in Wiltshire where the line of the outer bailey has left a half-oval shape in the modern street plan. The establishment of a strong castle automatically stimulated urban settlement in its vicinity; and it was often the baron in his castle who founded that essential nucleus of town life, the parish church. The church of St John, Devizes, which has a fine Norman tower, once lay within the inner bailey and served almost certainly as the castle chapel. Some towns such as Totnes and Launceston are still dominated by their castles, albeit in ruins, perched on lofty mottes.

During the early Middle Ages numerous towns or boroughs sprang into life, some as natural growths and others as artificial creations. Montacute was originally a planned borough of 1102 which was later enlarged, and was referred to around the middle of the thirteenth century as a *novo borgo*. The main boom in borough creation occurred in the century leading up to the Black Death of 1348. This fearful outbreak of bubonic plague was particularly devastating in the West Country. Over one third of the inhabitants of Bristol succumbed to the deadly disease, and in many manors in the Wessex region mortalities were in excess of 50 per cent. The Black Death is generally held responsible for the desertion of many villages but there were other factors at work, as at Bardolfston in Dorset where the switch from arable farming to large-scale sheep runs was the probable cause for the abandonment. It was worsening weather conditions which brought about the desertion of the settlement of Hound Tor on Dartmoor by the early fourteenth century, one of several marginal upland sites to be abandoned at this time. The visible stone remains of this isolated hamlet of tiny houses and barns clustered round a modest 'manor house' date to the beginning of the thirteenth century, but excavation has shown that occupation at Hound

Launceston, Cornwall has retained one of its medieval town gates.

Hound Tor on Dartmoor shows the complete layout of an abandoned medieval village remote from any present settlement.

Gold Hill in Shaftesbury, Dorset, has kept its medieval character as well as the extensive views over open countryside.

Prysten House, is the oldest dwelling in Plymouth, dating from the fifteenth century.

Tor extended back to the tenth century or even earlier when the houses were of turf and wattle. In outline the houses prefigure the typical layout of the Dartmoor longhouse with a living room at one end and a cattle byre at the other. The ruins of Hound Tor are a particularly evocative site, inspiring the visitor to reflect on the permanence of Dartmoor itself and the impermanence of human attempts to scratch a living from this exposed and unyielding environment.

Hound Tor, or 'Hundatorra', according to Domesday, was a manor in the possession of the Abbot of Tavistock, yet another instance of the ubiquitous presence of the Church in the Middle Ages. With its extensive landholdings both in town and country, the Church played a leading role in the urban development of the region and has left its mark in many towns and cities. At Glastonbury there survives a building known as the Tribunal of the fifteenth century which originally served as a court house to dispense justice to those living under the jurisdiction of the Abbot. Another secular offshoot of Glastonbury Abbey is the sixteenth-century George and Pilgrims Hotel, one of the most lavish hostelries of its day, which catered for the lucrative pilgrimage traffic attracted by the Arthurian relics. One of the earliest of town houses in the West Country, Kirkham House in Paignton, is thought to have been built in the late fourteenth century as a cleric's residence. The Prysten House of 1490 in Plymouth may have been used by the Augustinians prior to the Dissolution.

At Wells, Bishop Ralph of Shrewsbury initiated the most impressive of urban schemes in the 1340s when he built the Vicars' Close, an entire street of forty-two terraced houses to the north of the cathedral, complete with a Vicars' Hall. The chapel, front gardens and gates were added in the fifteenth century. Bishop Beckington provided the funds for the Chain Gate, a bridge that permitted the vicars choral to pass from the Close to the cathedral without setting foot on the street. This was motivated by the same desire, as apparent in the Vicars' Close itself, to isolate the clerics from the temptations of town life, to which they all too readily succumbed. At Exeter the Dean and Chapter rebuilt a tenement for leasing in the High Street at the end of the fourteenth century; and Abbey

The Glastonbury Tribunal was built by the abbey to try cases under its jurisdiction.

The range of sixteenth-century houses in Abbey Street, Cerne Abbas in Dorset, was probably built by the Benedictine monks.

Vicars Close, Wells, (right) *is a small masterpiece of medieval urbanism sponsored by the famous Bishop of Wells, Ralph of Shrewsbury.*

Street in Cerne Abbas may also have been a real estate development financed by the Abbey.

But the most comprehensive urban scheme of the Church was surely the creation of the entire town of New Sarum or Salisbury in the early thirteenth century. Although the original houses have long since been replaced, the squares or 'chequers' of the grid of six streets running east to west and five north to south have survived largely intact. In respect of its rational, rectilinear planning Salisbury stands apart from other medieval cities with their curved streets and twisting passages. Clarity of purpose was evident in the enterprise from the outset, for Bishop Richard Poore, the man who finally succeeded in having the see transferred from Old Sarum to the 'spacious fields and pleasantness' of Salisbury, was well aware that the economic prosperity of the town would be the best guarantee of the existence of the cathedral, to which the rents and market dues were payable. The two spheres of town and clerical gown were thus locked in an interdependence, with the Dean and Chapter reaping great benefit from the booming of the cloth trade in Salisbury. John à Port's timber-framed house of *c.* 1450 in Three Lyon Chequer, now a china emporium, and the hall of John Halle's house, an unexpected sight behind the façade of the Odeon cinema, are the main survivors of the town dwellings of Salisbury's wealthy wool merchants of the late medieval period.

Throughout the Middle Ages the export of woollen cloth and the import of luxury goods such as wine from the Continent brought prosperity to many towns and cities in the West Country, most notably Bristol and Exeter. Despite the heavy toll taken by both redevelopment over the centuries and air raids during the last war, a number of old buildings remain. The Exeter Guildhall ranks as the oldest functioning municipal premises in the country, with a history extending back to 1160; but the hall itself dates from 1330 and has undergone a series of modifications. The magnificent oak roof was installed in 1468, and the flamboyant Elizabethan portico was an addition of 1592–4. An even closer link to the wool trade which established the fortunes of Exeter is the Hall of the Weavers, Fullers and Shearmen of 1471 and known now as the Tuckers' Hall.

Sadly, little remains of the glory that was medieval Bristol, which by the middle of the fourteenth century was the leading English port for the export of woollen cloth. As a sign of its importance Bristol became a county in its own right in 1373, a metropolitan area wedged between the rural counties of Gloucestershire and Somerset, whose wool production was traded through the port on the Avon. The wealth of Bristol merchants in the Middle Ages was second only to London, and their charitable patronage has left its mark in an array of parish churches which still enhance the old city. Bristol Bridge was like London Bridge, with both sides lined with shops and houses; and like its more famous sister over the Thames it too has been replaced by a more conventional structure. Some last vestiges of medieval atmosphere may be sampled at the steep, winding passage known quaintly as Christmas Steps. Given the paucity of secular relics of the medieval townscape in Bristol it comes as a welcome surprise to enter the building known as Red Lodge which once commanded a fine view of the harbour full of ships with high masts riding the tides or sitting on the mud. This noble house of *c.* 1590 has been occupied by many Bristol merchant families over the years. The Great Oak Room is a marvel of oak panelling which is entered via a porch of magnificent carving in typically exuberant Renaissance style where the Classical motifs, applied with enthusiasm if without learning, conspire to beguile the onlooker. The upper half of the porch contains a wealth of heraldry and some carvings of half-figures of Red Indians, presumably a reference to Bristol's trade with America.

The Elizabethan House in Plymouth's Barbican has authentic period atmosphere.

More modest merchants' homes of the period are to be found elsewhere in the West Country in towns such as Dartmouth and Totnes. These, like the Merchant's House in St Andrew's Street, Plymouth, are now open to the public as museums. Most evocative of all is the Elizabethan House in New Street in the Barbican district of Plymouth. This was part of a late sixteenth-century development of some thirty houses for ships' captains and merchants of the middling sort. The crooked timbers of the building creak at every step, and the rooms are as snug and cosy as the cabins aboard ship. The Barbican is especially delightful because some of the ancient narrow streets, within sight and smell of the sea, have retained their original character. From the upper storey of the Elizabethan House you can reach out and shake hands with your neighbour on the opposite side of New Street. It was just this informal intimacy of the medieval hugger-mugger which was swept aside by the Classical revolution in urbanism which hit the region at the beginning of the eighteenth century.

Towns such as Frome in Somerset had been growing as a result of the increasingly

The Exchange by John Wood marks one of the highpoints of the Classical transformation of Bristol in the eighteenth century.

The spire of St Nicholas, Bristol, (left) viewed down an alleyway from Corn Street affords a partial impression of the medieval city which survives but in fragments.

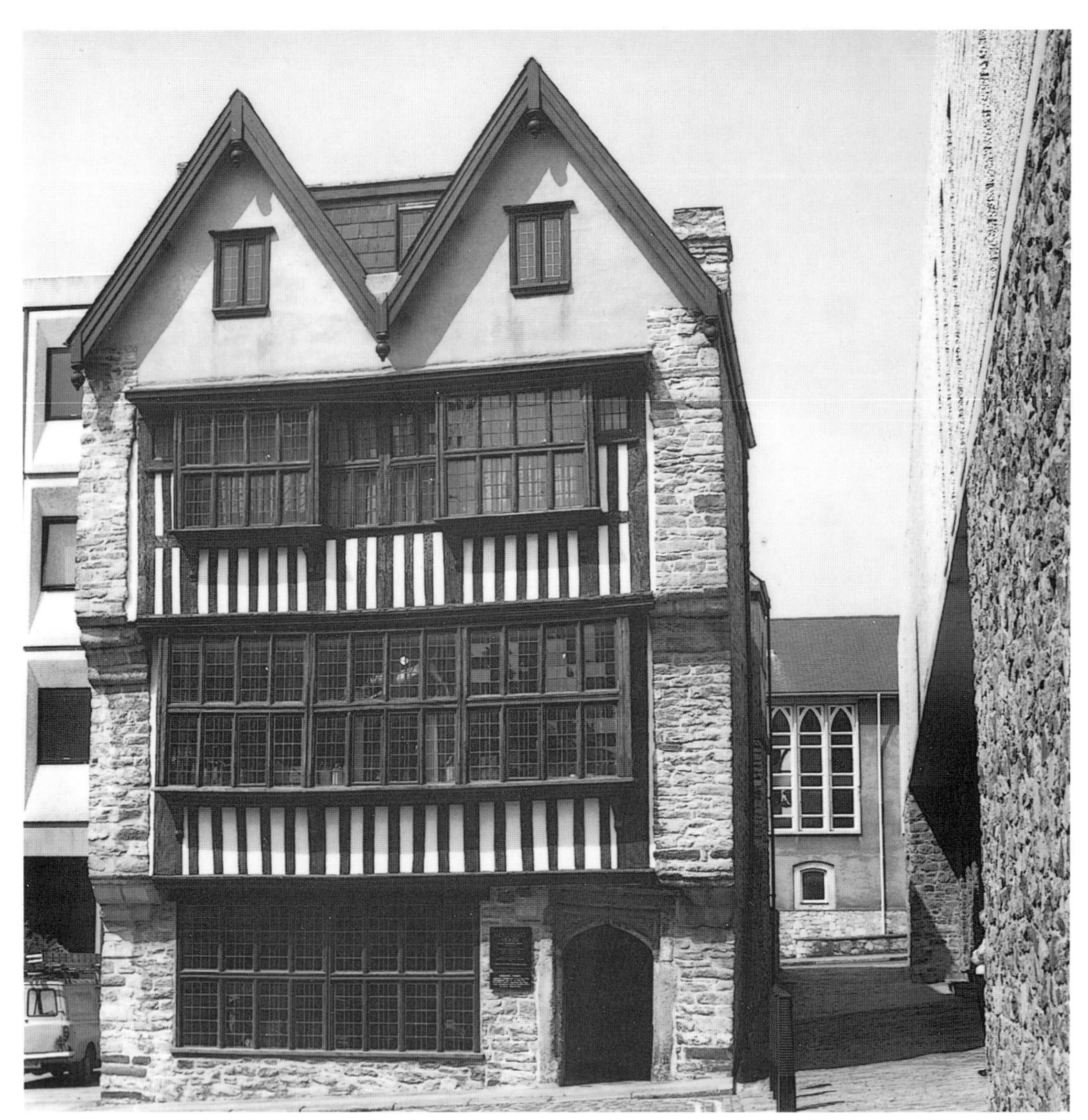

The sixteenth-century Merchant's House in Plymouth now serves as a museum.

centralised manufacture of the cloth industry; its population of rateable inhabitants had quadrupled in the last forty years of the seventeenth century. A new suburb was laid out to accommodate this demographic explosion of weavers. By about 1724 Daniel Defoe could report that the population had 'prodigiously increased through the last twenty or thirty years and is now higher than that of Bath and even Salisbury'. The Trinity area of Frome remains as one of the most important enclaves of workers' housing of its period. Greater opulence is on display at Trowbridge in Wiltshire where the clothiers' town mansions in The Parade resemble miniature palaces. The wealth of the clothiers is also much in evidence at Bradford-on-Avon where, alongside the humbler dwellings of the weavers, there arose stately, Classical town mansions for the successful clothiers such as Westbury House and Druce's Hill House. However,

Bradford-on-Avon remains a medieval town clinging to its hills, and its Georgian houses are not in a Georgian setting. The same applies to Blandford Forum in Dorset, which was totally rebuilt after a devastating fire of 1731. The houses and public buildings, designed by the brothers John and William Bastard, are resolutely Classical – if not correct according to the canons of Palladianism – but the street pattern of the house adheres obdurately to the medieval precursor on the site.

The orderly expansion of Bristol during its commercial golden age began as early as the 1650s with King Street, where it is instructive to look at a surviving building of *c.* 1665 known as Llandoger Trow. Its timber-frame and gabled front represent a last flourish of medieval style, before a more orderly type of architecture took over in Queen Square from 1699. It was here that a new type of Classical town house was introduced to Bristol in a style confident but provincial; and several houses of the first generation still convey a partial impression of the general effect. But the overall harmony of the square has been ruined by redevelopment and the diagonal gash of the Redcliffe Way, which has left the statue of King William III oddly marooned in the middle between the two lanes of traffic. In its day Queen Square was in the vanguard of a revolution in urban planning and was soon to be followed in Bristol by the laying out of St James's Square in 1707. But Bristol's Georgian beginnings were about to be put in the shade by the aristocratic elegance of Bath. Just before that happened, however, the modest Somerset town of Bridgwater managed to score an architectural 'first' by creating in Castle Street of 1723 an entire street conceived as a single stylistic unity, with generous five-bay town houses presenting a unified architectural façade. The grandiose scheme was due to the vision of its noble patron and owner of the land, the Duke of Chandos. But whatever its significance as an act of pioneering urbanism, Castle Street in Bridgwater was but the merest hint of what was about to be achieved at Bath.

Despite the existence of its hot springs which had made Bath one of the leading spa towns of the Roman Empire, the city had never recovered its metropolitan sophistication. It was still essentially a medieval walled city with a population of some 2000 at the end of the seventeenth century. The baths were in use, but the conditions, as described later around the middle of the eighteenth century by John Wood, were horrific: 'The Baths were like so many Bear Gardens, and Modesty was entirely shut out of them; People of both Sexes bathing by Day and Night naked; and Dogs, Cats, and even human creatures were hurl'd over the rails into the water, while People were bathing in it.' John Wood, the master architect of the new Bath, had a natural vested interest in overstating the case, but there was undoubtedly much truth in his description. As for the town itself, Wood wrote:

> The streets and public ways of the city were become like so much dunghills, slaughter house, pig styes: for soil of all sorts, and even carrion, were cast and laid in the streets, and the pigs turned out by day to feed and rout among it; butchers killed and dressed their cattle at their own doors; people washed every kind of thing they had to make clean at the common conduits in the open streets; and nothing was more common than small racks and mangers at almost every door for the baiting of horses.

Into this slum of an urban farmyard there strode at the beginning of the eighteenth century the unlikely, dandified figure of Beau Nash, probably with a perfumed handkerchief held to his nose, who was to set in motion a complete Renaissance of the city which elevated Bath to the rank of Georgian city *par excellence* in Britain as a whole.

Nash became Master of Ceremonies in 1704; and, making the most of the royal patronage extended by Queen Anne in 1702 and 1703, he transformed Bath into a centre

Cavendish Crescent (above) *and Royal Crescent* (right) *exemplify the tenets of Classical eighteenth-century urban planning which have made Bath the Georgian city* par excellence.

of style, fashion and elegance, offering all the facilities demanded by the leisured, aristocratic society of the day. Defoe documented the change: 'In former times this was a resort hither for cripples . . . but now we may say it is the resort of the sound, rather than the sick; the bathing is made more a sport and a diversion, than a physical prescription for health; and the town is taken up in raffling, gameing, visiting, and in a word, all sorts of gallantry and levity.' This was accompanied by an architectural transformation which gave Bath's noble visitors a setting worthy of their self-image.

John Wood began the urban metamorphosis soon after his arrival in Bath in 1727 with the building of Queen Square from 1729, which amounted to the very first palatial design of an English square, a generation in advance of even London. The Parades followed in 1740, but it was not until 1754, the year of John Wood's death, that one of his most original creations, the Circus, was begun. This has been described as following the elliptical shape of the Colosseum in Rome, but inverted to form an outer shell of thirty-three town houses held together in one sweeping composition by their unified frontages of three superimposed orders. The Circus was just part of a much grander vision which John Wood had dreamed of realising: 'In each design I proposed to make a grand Place of Assembly, to be called the Royal Forum of Bath; another place, no less magnificent, for the Exhibition of Sports, to be called the Grand Circus; and a third Place, of equal status with either of the former, for the Practice of Medicinal Exercises, to be called the Imperial Gymnasium.' John Wood the Younger continued the work of his father to complete the Circus, and in 1766 he began that most successful prototype of urban compositions in England, the Royal Crescent, which has been imitated in so many lesser forms throughout the country. Bath continued to build right into the nineteenth century and acquired such fine works of architecture as Robert Adam's Palladian Pulteney Bridge of 1774 giving access to the new suburb of Bathwick. By 1801 the population had reached 28,000, a fourteen-fold increase in just 100 years. But of all the wonders of eighteenth-century Bath, the Royal Crescent remains the most spectacular, standing for an entirely fresh concept in urban design, a combination of Palladian formality set like a jewel in a Picturesque landscape brought into the heart of town. An enticing glimpse of the internal elegance of Georgian Bath is afforded by the house at number 1 Royal Crescent which is open to the public.

Thus Bath's aristocratic allure conspired to hold the architectural supremacy over commercial Bristol throughout the eighteenth century, although Bristol did acquire its finest Georgian building, The Exchange of 1743, from the drawing board of John Wood the Elder. This noble Palladian structure in Corn Street was later abandoned by most of the merchant community in 1811 with the opening of the Commercial Rooms. Behind its austere Ionic portico, also in Corn Street, the original interior of the Grand Coffee Room is still intact beneath its sky-lighted dome. A central feature is the wind dial, activated by a weather-vane on top of the building, which permitted the merchants to judge when it was convenient for shipping to enter or to leave the port. The old city remained the commercial hub of Bristol throughout the nineteenth and into the twentieth century. Despite the decline in activity brought about by competition from Liverpool as a transatlantic port, Bristol was still sanguine enough in 1903 to commission a new building for its Stock Exchange, a very late appearance of florid, Italianate design, not much admired by the critics, but possessed of an endearing Edwardian optimism.

Bristol's new suburb of Clifton exploited the natural slope of its site to create a series of terraces, squares and crescents to challenge those of Bath. Royal York Crescent, reputedly the longest in Europe, and the double-fronted crescent Paragon of 1813

The elegant doorway of a town house in Bath's Lansdown Crescent.

are the most impressive of their type in Bristol, but they cannot quite match the splendour of Bath's Royal Crescent. Clifton eventually acquired its own Assembly Rooms in 1806, but the attempt to set up a fashionable spa at Hotwells failed to attract the fashionable set which made the fortunes of Bath; most of Clifton was inhabited by the wealthier folk of Bristol rather than by noble visitors. A typical house of the period which may be visited is the Georgian house at number 7 Great George Street, a building of 1790 which conveys the refined but solid comfort enjoyed by Bristolians with adequate means at that time. The medieval heart of the city was not obliterated as at Bath but lived on through the boom years of the eighteenth century. The Bristol wine firm of John Harvey was content to base its enterprise in a building over the cellars once belonging to the Augustinian Abbey. The ancient monastic vaults were used to store the barrels of port and sherry which were dragged up directly from

Royal York Crescent, Bristol, lacks the stately refinement of the nobler productions of this type in Bath, but it makes up for it in sheer size and claims to be the longest crescent in the whole of Europe.

The Paragon is one of Bristol's most successful set-pieces of urban development.

the waterfront over the cobbles of Denmark Street. The quayside is now an ordinary road, but the cellars are still owned by the company and now house Harveys Wine Museum.

Although Bath and Bristol commanded the centre-stage in the eighteenth century, there were other notable instances of Georgian classicism in towns and cities throughout the region. Taunton's Hammet Street of 1788 aligns itself perfectly on the glorious medieval tower of St Mary Magdalene, and the town acquired its almost obligatory crescent in 1807. Southernhay in Exeter and Lemon Street in Truro are delightful essays in the provincial Georgian style. Regency architecture, which added a welcome note of levity and fantasy to the formality of Georgian, was a natural style for the new rash of seaside resorts which spread along the coast of the West Country in the nineteenth century such as Torquay, Sidmouth, Weymouth, Ilfracombe and Newquay.

The heavy hand of Victorian commercial and civic architecture has left its mark in the West Country as elsewhere with its familiar array of banks, town halls, schools, public libraries, factories and warehouses. There will be found little in these buildings to suggest any strong regional identity. With the opening of the canals and railways, dependence on locally quarried stone became a thing of the past. Brickworks could now send their products to places previously remote, so that buildings of broadly similar character were constructed in all corners of the kingdom. Nevertheless, Bristol managed to develop a style of its own in its impressive warehouses which has been defined as 'Bristol Byzantine'; the finest surviving example of the genre is the Welsh Back Granary of 1869. This ten-storey 'palazzo' of red brick, relieved by bands of black and yellow and topped by Guelfic battlements reminiscent of Venice, is a truly noble edifice to crown the urban achievements of the entire region.

The Welsh Back Granary in Bristol was a brave exponent of the new industrial style.

This clapper-bridge at Postbridge on Dartmoor eased the progress of packhorse traffic.

The Industrial Past

A picture of industrial activity in the West Country some 500 years ago could well be conveyed by the peaceful scene of vast flocks of sheep grazing the hills, for it was the basic commodity of wool which made the early fortunes of the region. In fact, the production of woollen cloth goes back to the Neolithic peoples who introduced the arts of spinning and weaving to these shores over 5000 years ago. The need for warm clothing came very high on the list of priorities along with weapons and food vessels. It was not until the Middle Ages, however, that wool production became an organised industrial activity which yielded a cash surplus that could be spent on a variety of cultural refinements and material comforts, most notably fine buildings.

The Cistercians, anxious to derive an income from their extensive but remote landholdings, discovered that sheep were the best cash crop; and it was the white monks who pioneered the wool production in the early Middle Ages which was to contribute greatly to the conversion of huge tracts of arable land to pasture. On Dartmoor the tracks between the Cistercian abbeys of Buckfast and Tavistock and other centres may be described as the industrial arteries of the day, for they were used for the traffic of bundles of wool carried on the backs of pack-horses. Streams were forded wherever possible, but in places clapper bridges were constructed from the huge slabs of moorstone which lay on the surface of the moor. The most impressive of Dartmoor's clapper bridges is at Postbridge, still well maintained after more than 600 years; and there is another at Dartmeet, which has fallen into some dilapidation.

At the outset, the production cycle of wool was entirely domestic, from the sheep farmers to a chain of cottage industrialists composed of carders, spinners and weavers. The last two activities were concentrated in the cities such as Bristol, Exeter and Salisbury as well as in a variety of towns whose names are commemorated in the types of woollen cloth they produced, such as Barnstaple bays, Tavistock friezes and Totnes pinwhites. Fleeces were stored in great barns such as that in Bradford-on-Avon; and it takes nothing away from the splendour of this building to view it as a relic of medieval industrial archaeology.

Although spinning and weaving were to remain as cottage industries for several centuries, the process of fulling the wool was revolutionised by the use of water power at specially designed mills. These were situated by fast flowing rivers away from the urban centres, which, with the exception of Salisbury, saw their manufacturing role decline. Bristol and Exeter continued to prosper on the profits of the export trade, and by around 1500 more than 10,000 cloths were being shipped through Exeter every year. The spinners and weavers settled increasingly near the new fulling mills, and thus towns such as Bradford-on-Avon, Frome, Shepton Mallet and Warminster sprang into prominence. Along the banks of the Frome occurred the greatest concentration of fulling mills. There are still firm traces of the numerous leats and weirs which channelled the waters of the Frome to the mill wheels.

The manufacture of West Country broadcloth was greatly encouraged by the tax system which imposed a heavy duty on the export of the raw material. Commercial success was also due to the enterprise of the clothiers, the capitalists of their time, who financed the entire trade from the sheep's back to the ship's hold. Their fine

Abbey Mill at Bradford-on-Avon aimed to reverse the decline in cloth production.

houses are still a great feature of towns such as Trowbridge and Bradford-on-Avon, but they also aspired to country mansions such as South Wraxall and Corsham Court in Wiltshire. Money was lavished not just on churches, as has been described, but also on almshouses and schools such as the famous establishment at Tiverton founded in 1604 by Peter Blundell. Export of the broadcloth was mainly to Europe for dyeing and finishing. Much of the Exeter trade passed through the small port of Topsham to the Low Countries, and this trading link has left its mark in the neat Dutch gables of the merchants' houses. The wool industry may be detected also in some unlikely places, as at the medieval George Inn at Norton St Philip in Somerset built by Hinton Priory. According to tradition the woolmen used to meet in the upper rooms of the inn to discuss prices.

Domestic weaving in the West Country continued right into the eighteenth century, although one William Stumpe of Malmesbury did make an early move into factory production when he installed large looms in the nave of the abbey church at Malmesbury, which he acquired at the Dissolution. Marks left on the masonry are said to be the result of Stumpe's factory venture, but the energetic clothier more than compensated for any sacrilege by subsequently making over the church to the people of Malmesbury for parochial use. It is strange to imagine the scene at Malmesbury Abbey just over 400 years ago with William Stumpe's great looms prefiguring the industrial age within the carcass of an ancient Norman church.

Textile manufacture was central to the economy of the West Country until well into the nineteenth century, but by the end of the eighteenth regional supremacy had already passed to Yorkshire and Lancashire. The West Country did maintain its high standard of quality and specialisation in materials such as serge, which was centred in the towns of Taunton and Tiverton of the Devon-Somerset borders; but the persistence with heavy, expensive cloth when the way ahead lay with the cheaper, lighter worsteds for the emerging mass market, undermined the viability of the industry which lurched from crisis to crisis. Bradford-on-Avon attempted to fight back in 1875 with the construction of the palatial Abbey Mill, one of the largest in the region, but this did not survive for long as an active enterprise. The magnificent building was eventually converted into offices and a restaurant in 1968–72. Avon Mill at Malmesbury, another fine industrial structure, has been rescued for residential occupation. Coldharbour Mill at Uffculme in Devon, which ceased production as recently as 1981, has been kept going through the efforts of the Coldharbour Mill Trust as a working wool museum which still carries out a limited amount of spinning and weaving.

If wool is the most ancient industrial activity of the West Country, then the most thoroughly industrial in the modern sense is mining, for this brought with it the development and manufacture of heavy machinery and pressed its workers into living conditions every bit as horrific as the notorious areas of the Black Country and the North. The boom in mining belongs firmly to the nineteenth century, but the extraction of metal ores in the region goes back at least 2000 years. The theory that the Phoenicians came to Cornwall to purchase tin cannot be proven archaeologically, but there is firm evidence of Roman interest in the Cornish sources of tin from the middle of the third century AD after the Spanish tin mines had become exhausted. It would seem also that the Romans had prior knowledge of the lead deposits on Mendip, for a lead ingot stamped with the name of Claudius was produced from the Mendip deposits just a few years after the Roman invasion. It is difficult to identify with certainty the Roman workings at Charterhouse-on-Mendip from the other 'gruffy ground' caused by the surface upcast, for lead mining continued intermittently for several centuries and was a source of great wealth in the locality. The noble tower of St Mary Magdalen, Chewton Mendip, was financed by the profits from lead, not from wool as might be expected. Silver, often mined in association with lead, also has an ancient history. The silver-lead mines of the Tamar Valley are as old as any in England, and their discovery is generally dated to the end of the thirteenth century. Of similar antiquity are the silver mines at Combe Martin on the north Devon coast. It is recorded that Edward I brought miners from Derbyshire and Wales to work the Devon deposits. Combe Martin provided a dowry of 270lb of silver on the occasion of the marriage of Edward I's daughter Eleanor.

Tin mining in Devon and Cornwall was for centuries not really a mining activity at all. The ore or 'black tin' was readily available on the surface in the form of cassiterite pebbles covered by lighter alluvial deposits. There are many traces, especially on Dartmoor, of medieval streaming for tin which cast up heaps of rubble waste, now overgrown, along the banks of the stream. 'Leats' or water channels were created to wash away the debris and reveal the heavier cassiterite pebbles lurking beneath. The ore was then crushed and smelted in blowing-houses of stone and turf, and on Dartmoor alone some seventy sites of such structures have been identified such as the two at Black Tor Falls on the River Meavey.

Shaft-mining remained a difficult undertaking until the eighteenth century due to

Paper making from rags was an offshoot of the textile business. At Wookey Hole there is a rare surviving rag boiler (right) *which reduces the fibre to a wet pulp, from which paper is still made by hand with the aid of wooden frames* (above).

steam
water

One of Thomas Newcomen's atmospheric engines is preserved in Dartmouth, Devon.

the constant flooding of the mines. The problem was first tackled by the use of water-driven and horse-operated pumps as described by Richard Carew in his 'Survey of Cornwall' at the very end of the sixteenth century: 'For conveying away the water, they (the miners) pray in aid of sundry devices such as addits, pumps and wheels, driven by a stream; all which not withstanding, the springs so encroach upon these inventions, that they are driven to keep men and somewhere horses at work both day and night without ceasing.' It was Thomas Newcomen (1663–1729), a toolmaker of Dartmouth supplying the Cornish miners, who invented the atmospheric engine which greatly facilitated the pumping-out of the mines. It relied on a low pressure of steam which was condensed in the cylinder by a jet of cold water; the pressure of the atmosphere on the resulting vacuum did the rest by forcing down the piston and thus raising the pump rod attached to the other end of the horizontal beam. But Newcomen's engine was inefficient, consuming vast quantities of coal which had to be imported into Cornwall at considerable expense. Not surprisingly, the Newcomen engine found greater application in the Midlands where the necessary fuel lay close at hand. One of the surviving Newcomen engines was brought to Dartmouth, the native town of the inventor, to celebrate the 300th anniversary of his birth.

The way ahead was shown by James Watt, inventor of the steam engine with separate condenser, which saved up to 75 per cent in fuel consumption. Watt's engine, patented in 1765 and developed in association with Matthew Boulton, was sold extensively in Cornwall, but the high engine dues payable before the patents expired in 1800 were much resented by the owners of the Cornish mines. Watt, for his part, has left us with a bitter description of the adventurers who ran Wheal Virgin ('wheal' means a 'working' or a 'mine' in Cornish) as 'a mean dirty pack, preying one upon another and striving who shall impose most upon the mine'. Watt's engines were later improved by the genius of the Cornishman Richard Trevithick (1771–1813) whose use of high pressure steam brought about the development of the enormous Cornish beam engine which became the industrial trademark of the county. Two of the most impressive of the surviving Cornish beam engines are now in the care of the National Trust at East Pool near Camborne-Redruth. The East Pool Whim is a winding engine for the raising and lowering of men and materials in the shaft and was designed in 1887. Not far away is the East Pool Pumping Engine of 1891–2, a monster of a machine of the largest size in use at the end of the nineteenth century.

Despite the efficiency of the new generation of beam engines, the tin-mining industry in Cornwall was not protected from a series of crises which were triggered off by dramatic fluctuations in the price of tin on the world market. Atrocious working conditions and starvation wages forced many Cornish miners to seek their fortunes in the notoriously dangerous mines of South America as well as in Australia. When mine closure created mass unemployment, the tide of emigration turned into a flood. In the 1830s and '40s tens of thousands of Cornishmen left their native soil to work in mines all over the world. Although there was partial recovery in the 1870s, the general trend was of remorseless decline, as witnessed today by the numerous abandoned engine houses which once served busy mines with evocative names such as Ding Dong, Botallack, Levant and Wheal Vor. Today these are but a few of the entries on the lengthy inventory of 'knacked bals' or disused mines. The sight of their tall, round chimneys, filled with nothing but the

East Pool Whim, a winding engine of 1887 vintage.

*A characteristic feature of the Cornish landscape are the tall chimneys of the abandoned engine houses which once served the tin mines in the county. Among the most spectacular are those on the coast such as Towanroath (*left*) and Botallack (*above*) where the tunnels extend far out to sea beneath the ocean bed.*

Morwellham Quay on the River Tamar was once a hive of industrial activity.

whistling wind, calls to mind the whole saga of tin mining, but the real mining heritage lies underground in the hundreds of miles of tunnels and shafts, which are only rarely accessible, as at Poldark Mine at Wendron. Many mine workings extend far out beneath the sea, where you can hear the pounding of the Atlantic which grinds huge boulders on the ocean floor, as a continuous background rumbling through the solid rock.

Tin mining still survives in Cornwall, albeit at a much reduced level, representing an unbroken tradition of some 2000 years. The story of copper mining in the West Country, on the other hand, was but a transient phenomenon which ran its course during the comparatively short period of just 200 years. However, in its heyday from 1750 to 1850 copper was vastly more valuable to Cornwall and Devon than tin. Copper production rose steadily during the early decades of the nineteenth century, but with the discovery in 1844 in the Tamar Valley of the richest ever copper lode things really took off. The mining company known as the Devon Great Consols was to break all records. Within little more than a year the value of a £1 share had rocketed to a phenomenal £800. This 'mine of mines', as it was once described, lay on land belonging to the Duke of Bedford, whose forbears had acquired this valuable property once held by the Abbey of Tavistock as part of the spoils of the Dissolution. Now, after more than 300 years, the investment was to show a spectacular return. The 6th Duke of Bedford had wanted 'no gang of miners disturbing his pheasants', but the 7th Duke was more amenable and received his reward with a veritable showering of wealth in royalties. When in 1903 the Devon Great Consols finally ceased production, the Duke of Bedford was so efficient in restoring the landscape for his cherished pheasant coverts that little now remains to indicate the site of England's greatest copper mine. The rebuilding of the centre of Tavistock, financed from the profits of the Devon Great Consols, is just a small indication of the immense wealth that was once generated.

The extent of the mighty enterprise can best be gauged from the restored ruins of Morwellham, the port on the Tamar which was developed to handle the export of the copper ore. The ore was brought to the quayside via the newly built Tavistock Canal and an incline railway. The tell-tale green deposit of the copper can still be seen on the old ore shutes, whence it was transported in trucks to the tile-covered ore floors pending shipment. Around the middle of the last century the Tamar was busier than the Mersey, for this now-sleepy river carried Europe's main supply of copper at that time. Arsenic was also produced, and became especially important after the

Copper ore from the Devon Great Consols was loaded at Morwellham Quay for shipment.

The extraction of China clay, which occurs in granite areas, was achieved through the use of settling pits such as this one at Wheal Martyn in Cornwall.

The Haytor Railway on Dartmoor (left) *used tracks of solid granite for the transport of huge blocks of granite extracted from the nearby quarry.*

decline in copper set in around 1865–70. Morwellham today presents itself as a spruce industrial heritage site, and it is difficult to imagine the scene just 100 years ago when this was one of the most industrialised places in England, a hive of human toil under a sky dark with poisonous pollution.

Possessing none of the glamour of tin or copper, the extraction of china clay has now come to displace in importance the mining for those metals in the West Country. The substance known as china clay or 'kaolin', the essential ingredient for making true porcelain, occurs as a natural product in granite areas as a result of a decomposition of the feldspar component of granite by a process known as 'kaolinisation'. The vast granite uplands of Devon and Cornwall all contain huge deposits of kaolin and of that other important product china stone, but the secret of these hidden riches was unsuspected until almost the middle of the eighteenth century. The Chinese, who knew all about the geology most likely to yield china clay, kept the source of their own supply shrouded in secrecy as best they could.

The presence of kaolin in the West Country was at last detected by the chemist William Cookworthy (1705–80), a Quaker of Kingsbridge in Devon, who first discovered quantities of the material in the 1740s in Tregonnin Hill. Surprisingly, it was not until 1768 that Cookworthy finally applied for a patent to manufacture 'a kind of porcelain newly invented by me composed of moor-stone or growan [china clay], and growan clay [china clay]'. Cookworthy's first venture was the Plymouth China Factory, but the enterprise was moved in 1770 to Bristol, and the patent was taken over by Richard Champion. For a while the patent prevented other potters such as Josiah Wedgwood from using kaolin in their own manufacture, but the monopoly was soon broken and china clay from Cornwall was exported not just to the Midlands but to the Continent as well. Wedgwood actually planned to establish a pottery in Cornwall close to the source of the raw material, but the cost of importing coal to fire the kilns was a serious deterrent. It was cheaper to transport the china clay rather than the coal, and a number of ports were built to service this trade. The harbour at Charlestown, commenced in 1791, was followed in 1829–40 by the entirely artificial harbour at Par, which took over the lead from Charlestown later in the nineteenth century. Fowey became the greatest of all the china-clay ports, thanks to its ability to receive ocean-going vessels and its convenient location for the numerous china-clay pits on the Hensbarrow. The 'great white road to Fowey' so called on account of the traces of china clay it has collected, is still an economic reality.

The most obvious physical relics of the china-clay industry are the flooded pits where the minute particles of china clay, held in suspension, give the still waters a hue of brilliant turquoise. Together with the conical waste-tips, many of which are overgrown with wild rhododendron, the blue lakes conspire to create a landscape of surrealist qualities. The best place to obtain an overall view of the china clay industry of the past as well as a spectacular vista of modern methods using earthmovers is at Wheal Martyn near St Austell. Workings such as these helped lift the periodic economic depressions of Cornwall and employed many miners made redundant by the tin and copper crises, thereby ensuring the survival of an industrial base in the county right up to the present.

As for granite, the parent material of china clay, it too became the subject of a quarrying industry in the nineteenth century when at last the problems of transport could be overcome. The most ingenious of methods was employed at Haytor on Dartmoor where huge blocks of the granite itself were cut to form a granite railway. This 4-ft gauge track, incidentally the first railway in Devon, ran for 8½ miles from the quarry to a loading point on the Stover

A modern China clay working in operation at Wheal Martyn, Cornwall.

Canal at Teigngrace. The trucks were drawn along this novel railway by teams of horses; for steep sections as many as eighteen strong shires were held in readiness. Junctions in the line were provided by points that were actually carved out of the granite blocks. The points and sections of track from this megalithic railway are still clearly visible at Haytor; and the quarry itself, now flooded, appears to have turned itself into a miniature aquatic nature reserve, a secret enclave enclosed in granite on one of the windswept hilltops of Dartmoor. Haytor granite was used extensively for a hundred years from 1820 to about 1920, most notably for the foundation stone of London Bridge in 1825. Granite is still extracted from Dartmoor at the Tor Quarry near Merrivale.

The transport of heavy materials such as granite from Haytor was only made possible by the building of a network of canals which enjoyed a brief moment of glory before the coming of the railways sparked off another transport revolution. Although 'canalomania' properly belongs to the eighteenth century, the West Country had already pioneered artificial waterways as

The noble Dundas Aqueduct near Bath confers architectural dignity on a work of engineering designed to carry the Kennet and Avon Canal over the River Avon.

One of the wonders of the canal age in Britain was the great flight of locks which enabled the Kennet and Avon Canal to negotiate the hilly terrain at Devizes in Wiltshire.

early as 1563–6 when the first Exeter Canal was dug to circumvent the weirs on the River Exe. This was the first canal to be built in England since the departure of the Romans. In the course of four centuries of active service it has been improved several times, but this is basically the same waterway that, in the reign of Queen Elizabeth I, permitted shipping to penetrate inland as far as Exeter. The present canal basin, part of which houses the Exeter Maritime Museum, dates to 1830. The Exeter Canal, although much reduced in importance since the arrival of the railway at Exeter in 1844, has managed to keep open. This is in contrast to most other canal enterprises in the West Country which were ambitiously launched to serve a purpose soon to become redundant, or with little thought given to the real nature of the physical problems involved. As an example, the Bude Canal, authorised by Act of Parliament in 1774, was to have extended 95 miles inland via Launceston to Calstock, but only 35½ miles were built. Its main purpose was to carry shelly sand, a useful addition to acid soil, into the farming country of the hinterland. The tracks of a narrow gauge railway leading from the beach at Bude to the side of the canal are still in place, but the Bude Canal itself extends inland only a few miles and is used now exclusively by pleasure boats.

The Great Western Maritime Ship Canal was intended to permit the transport of coal from south Wales via Bridgwater Bay on the Bristol Channel to Exmouth on the south Devon coast, but the project was not to be realised. In 1792 there was a scheme for the Grand Western Canal to link the River Exe to Taunton and thence to Bristol. Work began in 1796, and a waterway between Tiverton and Taunton was opened in 1838, but the project was never completed. A beautiful section of the canal at Tiverton is now operated by horse-drawn barges. More successful, though also short-lived, was the Kennet and Avon Canal of 1810. It linked up with the Avon Navigation from Bath to Bristol, which enabled Ralph Allen to transport Bath stone from his quarry at Combe Down, and extended the waterway fifty-seven miles to the east via Devizes and Hungerford to Newbury and Reading on the Thames, thereby providing a route for canal boats between Bristol and London. The Kennet and Avon was a generous 40 ft wide and included 79 locks along its course; 29 of these are to be found in Devizes alone, where they climb the hill in a spectacular ladder formation. But even this triumph of engineering was not able to withstand for long the competition of Brunel's Great Western Railway, which not only captured the prestigious London to Bristol route, but soon extended its gleaming tracks like tentacles deep into the West Country, swallowing up other independent railway companies as it went.

The Great Western Railway was one of the most romantic institutions of the industrial era. Its choice of the charismatic Isambard Kingdom Brunel, designer of the Clifton Suspension Bridge, as engineer, and the persistence of the company with the 7 ft broad gauge while the standard gauge of 4 ft 8½ in had been generally accepted by the other companies, were both signs of the élitism which earned the GWR its nickname of 'God's Wonderful Railway'. However, the joke was turned neatly on its head by its detractors, who called it the 'Great Way Round' as an ironic reference to the need of the broad gauge to seek gentler gradients for its lines. The route between London and Bristol, authorised by the Act of 31 August 1835, was criticised on account of the lack of any significant commercial towns between Bath and Reading. Brunel's response that the GWR was 'a gentleman's railway' has passed into the annals of legend surrounding the company.

One of the greatest engineering achievements of the GWR was the two-mile tunnel driven under Box Hill between 1836–41, a Titanic struggle which ripped almost one quarter of a million cubic yards of Bath stone from the bowels of the hill. At the

Brunel's Saltash Bridge over the Tamar finally anchored Cornwall to the rest of England.

GENTS
THE GREAT TRAIN SHED
LONDON LIFE AND BRUNEL

Brunel's Torre Station in Torquay shows an elegant combination of iron and wood which was characteristic of the Great Western Railway.

Brunel's original Temple Meads station (left) *in Bristol has a wooden roof inspired by the hammerbeam constructions of the Middle Ages.*

height of the work about 4,000 men worked around the clock in shifts; and more than 100 labourers were killed and many more maimed in horrendous accidents. When completed, the tunnel was embellished by a palatial western entrance of Classical masonry. The fact that the passengers might only have caught a quick glimpse through the smoke of the noble portico as the train was engulfed by the darkness hardly mattered at all. What counted most was the spirit of the thing. Even today the view of the magnificent entrance to Box Tunnel from the roadside of the A4 just west of Corsham seems to encapsulate the romanticism of the early years of the railway era. Some Brunel fanatics claim that the sun shines directly through the tunnel on the birthday of the great engineer, but there is no substance to this delightful story.

The first headquarters of the GWR was at Bristol, the city which raised 60 per cent of the starting capital. Much survives of Brunel's original Temple Meads Station, in which the curious choice was made of Tudor Revival for an enterprise in the vanguard of industrial progress. Once the line from London was completed, the GWR extended the broad gauge to Exeter by 1844, and pushed ever further west into Devon and Cornwall, building such wonderful lines as the coastal railway from Exeter to Teignmouth, where in places there is little but the width of the track between the red cliffs and the blue sea. It was along this stretch of the old GWR that Brunel's ill-fated experiment with atmospheric traction took place. At Starcross stands an old pumping house next to the line; this was one of several which worked to create a vacuum in the iron tube which ran continuously between the rails. The resulting atmospheric pressure caused a piston to travel down the tube, pulling the train behind it. The system was scientifically sound, but there were terrible problems with the leather flap which kept the vacuum sealed while permitting the passage of the coupling between the piston and the train. The leather hardened after exposure to salt water or rotted, and in places was devoured by rats. A section of the abandoned line, known derisively as Brunel's 'atmospheric caper', is preserved at the Starcross Pumping House. A further humiliation for 'God's Wonderful Railway' occurred when the directors of the GWR were obliged to convert their entire network to the more practical standard gauge. A rare piece of original broad gauge has been put on display at Crowcombe Station in Somerset.

The GWR has had a dramatic and lasting effect on the West Country. It brought tourism to ports such as St Ives and Newquay and helped Newlyn to despatch its fish to Billingsgate overnight. Likewise it facilitated the marketing of agricultural produce such as fresh milk, and breathed new life into commercial centres from Salisbury to Exeter and Plymouth. But there was nothing quite so dramatic as the sudden transformation of Swindon in Wiltshire from a sleepy hamlet into a large industrial town. The decision to make Swindon the nerve-centre of the Great Western Railway sparked off an urban explosion. The original population of 1000 in 1801 had increased little before the GWR came to town in the 1840s, but by 1861 the figure had jumped to almost 7000 and was to double again by 1870. To cater for the influx of workers and to impose some disciplined way of life, a model village was built on a regular grid pattern based on eight streets which took their names from GWR stations such as Bath, Bristol, Exeter and Taunton. In all, 300 cottages were constructed; although restricted in size, they represented a considerable degree of comfort for their time. A lodging-house for single men was opened, which came to be known as 'The Barracks' for its regimented arrangements. The railway cottages are still in occupation, and one of them, at 34 Farringdon Road, has been restored to reflect the living conditions of the last

Interior of a worker's cottage in the purpose-built railway village at Swindon.

century. The Barracks now house the Great Western Railway Museum; and with the recent closure of the engineering works at Swindon by British Rail the town's pioneering railway days have passed away into the realm of history and heritage.

There was nothing quite like the Great Western Railway, and it came to symbolise so much of life in the West Country that its chocolate-and-cream livery conjured up visions of Devon and Cornwall even before the carriages had pulled out of Paddington. There is a statue of its greatest man, Isambard Kingdom Brunel, in Bristol, but a more moving tribute is the Royal Albert Bridge over the Tamar at Saltash. This records quite simply on a huge plaque: 'I. K. Brunel Engineer 1859'. Sadly, the designer of this mighty structure and of so much else for the GWR died just four months after the opening of the great bridge linking Cornwall to the rest of England.

Statue of Sir Francis Drake surveys Plymouth Sound from the legendary Hoe.

Maritime Heritage

What distinguishes the West Country from every other part of England is its deep and abiding relationship with the sea. Cornwall, in particular, is so much a maritime county that it is almost impossible to escape the sound and smell of the sea; the taste of salt in the air can penetrate, it would seem, even the upland fastness of Bodmin Moor. The River Tamar does its best to cut off the county and turn it into an island. Even though connected by land, Cornwall's communications with the rest of England until the improvement of the roads in the eighteenth century and the coming of the railway in the nineteenth were mainly by sea. Maritime routes were especially important in prehistoric times when Cornwall could be more accurately described as being part of an extensive Atlantic province which united the entire north-west fringe of Europe from Orkney and Shetland to Spain, although the unity was cultural rather than anything remotely political. The similarities in megalithic grave building between Brittany, Cornwall, Wales, Ireland and Scotland clearly demonstrate the movement of people across the seas. Thus, a tradition of intrepid seafaring extends back to the Neolithic and possibly the Mesolithic period, and it is a great shame that no archaeological evidence exists to indicate the type of boats used by these ancient peoples. There are historical references in the fourth century BC to the Britons taking to sea in craft of wickerwork covered with hide, now known chiefly by the survival of the Welsh coracle, but the prehistoric tribes must have built much larger versions, able to accommodate entire families and probably their livestock as well.

The sea must therefore be considered as a highway rather than as a barrier to progress, as in the case of the Saxons who used boats to establish a settlement in Brixham well in advance of the westward colonisation of Devon overland. But that must not be taken to mean that the ocean was ever regarded as a benign element. The passage around Land's End was always held in fear to the extent that two transpeninsular routes were usually preferred both by the Neolithic settlers and later by the Celtic saints. These can still be followed from St Ives' Bay to St Michael's Mount and from Padstow to Fowey. The perils of 'goin' roun' land', as they say in Cornwall, remain formidable. In 1855 a group of Bristol merchants, as a move against the expensive rates of the Great Western Railway, started a steamer service to London, which came to a tragic end when their vessel was wrecked, like so many others, off Land's End.

The folklore of the sea has a special mystery, such as the story woven around the lost land of Lyonesse said to lie submerged on the ocean floor between Cornwall and the Isles of Scilly. The legend relates that the knights who survived Arthur's last battle fled over Lyonesse to seek refuge in Scilly, and that a violent storm arose after their passage which swallowed up their enemies in hot pursuit, leaving Lyonesse under several fathoms of salt water ever since. As is so often the case with legends there is here too an element of physical reality; the submergence did occur, but the chronology is hopelessly wrong to fit the story. It has been calculated that the last time Scilly could have been reached over dry land was at least 10,000 years ago, rather than the mere 1,500 or so which separate us from Arthurian times. In any case, the rising of the sea level was a gradual process.

Mermaids are the most magical of all

The mermaid bench end at Zennor, Cornwall reflects a motif of maritime mythology.

creatures in maritime mythology, and there is none more so than the lascivious specimen carved on a bench-end in the church of St Senner at Zennor in Cornwall. One of the versions of the legend surrounding her is that she was enticed from her watery habitat by the divine singing of the local chorister Matthew Trewells. He in turn was so captivated by her beauty that he was lured away under the sea. His father ordered the carving to be made in the hope that the mermaid would be flattered by this tribute and be amenable to releasing his son. The woodcarver allowed himself full rein in his portrayal of feminine charm, but the ruse did not work and Matthew Trewells was never seen again.

Some of the people connected with the sea in the West Country assumed legendary proportions in their own lifetime. The intrepid seafarers of the Elizabethan age stand out not just as regional or even national figures, but as men who played a leading role on the world stage. Sir John Hawkins of Plymouth, scourge of the Spaniards and Portuguese, served as MP for Plymouth when he was not away at sea in search of loot and plunder. There was a less attractive side to his swashbuckling exploits, since Hawkins was one of the pioneers of the shameful traffic in slaves, on one occasion trading 300 blacks from Guineau for a rich cargo of pearls, hides, sugar and ginger in Haiti. His son Sir Richard Hawkins was also drawn to the two professions of privateering and parliament.

Sir Francis Drake, immortalised by his circumnavigation of the world and heroic exploits against the Spanish, is less well known in his more prosaic, municipal role as the Mayor of Plymouth who introduced such a basic improvement to the city as a fresh-water supply. A seventeen-mile-long leat was dug in 1591 to carry the waters of the River Meavy on Dartmoor all the way to Plymouth. It is said that Sir Francis marked the opening of the leat by riding ahead of the first surge of water on a white horse as if leading it symbolically into Plymouth. Drake also left his mark at Buckland Abbey, where his crest is to be found over the fireplace in the tower room, with other mementoes including his sword and his drum. Drake had acquired Buckland Abbey in 1581 from his seafaring colleague and rival Sir Richard Grenville, who had converted the old Cistercian monastery into a comfortable if somewhat eccentric country home. Grenville, the hero of the *Revenge*, was a native of Bideford on the north Devon coast; the town's park contains eight sixteenth-century Spanish cannons, presumed to be from the Armada.

Sir Walter Raleigh was born at Hayes Barton in East Budleigh in south Devon. The nearby seaside town of Budleigh Salterton was the setting chosen by John Millais for his famous painting *Boyhood of Raleigh*. One of Raleigh's contributions to the West Country was in promoting the splendid anchorage offered by Falmouth, a port which established itself in later centuries as a prosperous packet station. After his marriage to one of Elizabeth I's ladies-in-waiting he intended to set up home in the shell of Sherborne Old Castle in Dorset, a most unlikely setting for a sea-dog, but the conversion of the Norman buildings proved too ambitious an undertaking, and so Raleigh built a new house or lodge, as it was called, which still stands in the vicinity and bears the name of Sherborne Castle. It is of interest to note that the architecture of the Middle Ages was not despised by such a complete man of the Renaissance as Sir Walter Raleigh undoubtedly was.

The West Country abounds with memories of her great seafarers. Compton Castle in south Devon was the birthplace of Sir Humphrey Gilbert, one of the pioneers of colonisation in America, who led an abortive expedition to Florida but succeeded in 1583 in founding the English colony in Newfoundland, the first in North America. Compton Castle was repurchased by the Gilbert family in the 1930s and restored from a ruinous condition. One of the sons of the present occupants is actually named Walter Raleigh. Less well known are Stephen and William Burrough of Northam near Appledore who explored the Arctic coast of Russia in the sixteenth century, and whose name is commemorated in the Burrough Strait. The roll-call of West Country mariners could be extended by a whole list of privateers and adventurers from the Gallants of Fowey, the Killigrews of Falmouth, John Davis of Dartmouth among many others of that port, to John Oxenham of South Tawton whose South American adventure was taken up by Kingsley in his story *Westward Ho!*.

Behind this tradition of great seafarers there lies of course a much broader if less glamorous range of maritime activities such as fishing and trading which brought a measure of prosperity to many ports, large and small, around the coast of the peninsula. The earliest settlers would simply have chosen the most sheltered coves and estuaries, but with growing sophistication and human ingenuity harbours were improved or indeed created where none had previously existed. Mousehole in Cornwall, whose name refers to gulls rather than mice, was one of the earliest ports known to have built a pier. This was achieved at

Boscastle's snug harbour on the rugged north coast of Cornwall was once an active entrepôt which imported all the essential materials for the farms and mines of the hinterland. Its importance today depends largely on tourism.

the end of the fourteenth century and with the help of funds provided by the Crown. Mousehole was once one of the most important centres for fisheries, especially pilchards, and also served as the main departure point for pilgrims sailing to the Holy Land and to visit the shrine of St James of Compostela in Spain. Now it is just another of those pretty Cornish ports, much beloved on account of their picturesque intimacy, such as Polperro and Polkerris. One of the most visually pleasing of harbours is at Boscastle on the north coast of Cornwall. The pier, as rebuilt by Sir Richard Grenville in the 1580s, still enfolds the tiny port as if in the crook of a protective arm. The outer breakwater was constructed in about 1820 and has been rebuilt after being blown up by a floating mine in 1941. Without its daytrippers, who descend mainly on its Pixie Shop, Boscastle is a quiet place, but it was once a hive of activity as huge quantities of goods were shipped through this narrow passage in the rocks and hauled up the hill to the farms, villages and industrial centres of the hinterland. Clovelly's original harbour is of the same epoch, dating back to 1587. The picturesque appeal of its stepped main street where donkeys provide the haulage no longer needs the literary promotion provided in the last century by Dickens and Kingsley, whose stirring prose lured the first Victorian tourists to this remote place on the north Devon coast.

One of the most heroic of harbour works was at Hartland Quay on the most exposed shore of north Devon, facing head on into the full fury of the Atlantic. The daring enterprise was the initiative of William Abbot, whose great uncle had acquired the manor of Hartland at the Dissolution, and the work was carried out towards the end of the sixteenth century, a time of the most intense activity along the seaboard of the West Country. Laying the foundations could only be tackled at low water since the harbour at high tide lay under two fathoms of sea. The work was duly completed, but William Abbot died in 1609 before he had begun to see a proper return on his investment. Ownership of Hartland Quay then passed by marriage to the Luttrell family of Dunster who constructed a new pier at Minehead in 1616. Hartland Quay was subsequently leased to merchants and enjoyed a busy trade in the seventeenth and eighteenth centuries, and continued to thrive until 1841 when the pierhead was destroyed by a violent storm. It was rebuilt and then repaired on several occasions, but eventually in 1887 the pierhead was again demolished by the sea. The remaining part of the structure was almost entirely swept away in 1896, leaving behind just a stump of masonry as of an amputated limb. The foundations can still be seen at low tide, but the harbour as such no longer exists in any real sense, a grim reminder of the devastating power of the sea along these shores.

The most atmospheric of ports still operating mainly for fishing is Brixham; Sutton Harbour in Plymouth also maintains a small fishing fleet, although it is now given over mostly to the marina facilities required by pleasure craft. St Ives was once the great centre of pilchard fishing, exporting millions of the fish in barrels, with a large proportion going to Italy. The pilchard business reached a peak during the eighteenth and nineteenth centuries. Murray's *Handbook for Cornwall* noted of St Ives in 1851 that it was 'most abominably tainted with the effluvia of the fish cellars'. Such fish stores were commonplace in the ports of the region, but are scarcely recognisable today, now converted into shops, restaurants and residences. The first harbour breakwater at St Ives dates back to the end of the fifteenth century, and the new quay is of 1770 vintage.

Throughout the eighteenth and nineteenth centuries harbour improvements and rebuilding continued apace. A new port was built on the south Cornwall coast between 1792–8 by Charles Rashleigh, taking the name of its founder as Charlestown.

Brixham Harbour is still home to an enterprising trawling fleet.

The port enjoyed great prosperity through the pilchard fisheries and the export of copper and china clay. Pilchards and copper are no more, though china clay is still shipped to Europe through Charlestown; but the main activity now appears to be tourism, generated by the unique assemblage of eighteenth-century harbour installations, which include a four-gun battery on the headland built to deter the French. Bristol's 'Floating Harbour' was not built until the end of the eighteenth century, a time when the city was still involved in the horrific transportation of slaves from West Africa to the West Indies. Watchet, on the coast of Somerset, sprang into prominence in 1859 when the West Somerset Mineral Railway used it for shipping iron ore from the Brendon Hills to the smelters and foundries of south Wales. Further east along the Bristol Channel towards Weston-super-Mare, Brean Down was chosen as the site for an ambitious new trans-Atlantic port, aimed at restoring the business which Bristol had lost to Liverpool.

The prospectus of the Brean Down

(Overleaf) *The jagged rocks at Hartland Quay, Devon have claimed many a shipwreck.*

Smeaton's epoch-making lighthouse on the Eddystone Rocks was rebuilt on Plymouth Hoe.

Harbour and Railway Company was blithely confident: 'The Brean Down route to America will therefore be shorter both by land and sea than the existing route by Liverpool, and . . . will inevitably attract a large proportion of the American traffic. It is confidently anticipated that the Government must avail themselves of this Port when completed for the despatch of the Mails to America.' In reality, the port was not to be completed. The first stone was laid in 1864, but in 1872 a huge storm removed the stone pier, causing the abandonment of the project. There is little now to be seen at Brean Down but the remains of a fort constructed by the War Office.

It was the imperatives of war and defence which spurred on the development of both Portland Harbour in the mid nineteenth century and of Plymouth somewhat earlier. Plymouth had been a key naval base since the days of the Spanish Armada. The Royal Naval Dockyard at Devonport was founded in 1691 by William III, and the naval establishment there has been growing ever since. One of the most impressive buildings is the grand entrance to the Royal William Victualling Yard designed by the second John Rennie. The most spectacular part of the harbour works at Plymouth is the mighty breakwater out in the Sound, which provides vital protection from treacherous winds. This monumental work was created by the dumping of 3,620,444 tons of rubble on the sea bed between 1811 and 1847, a truly gigantic undertaking. The Breakwater Lighthouse was built from 1845 to crown what was one of the earliest of free-standing breakwaters to have withstood the test of time.

The natural hazards of the West Country coast made the provision of lighthouses an urgent priority. In the Middle Ages these were often quite modest affairs, as at Ilfracombe where the tiny chapel of St Nicholas on Lantern Hill kept a light burning to mark the narrow harbour entrance. Homespun installations were of no avail when it came to warning mariners of such dreadful dangers as the Eddystone Rocks, a 600-yard-long reef of jagged granite, mostly submerged, located fourteen miles south of Plymouth and exposed to the full fury of the Atlantic. Soon after William of Orange had chosen Plymouth as the site of his naval arsenal, the first attempt was made to put a lighthouse on the Eddystone Rocks, and in 1696 the candles were lit, but this iron structure was swept away in 1703 together with its unfortunate engineer. A new tower was erected but its timber succumbed to a fire, so a totally fresh start was made by John Smeaton, who designed a revolutionary type of lighthouse which became the prototype for most of those that were to follow. Smeaton's Tower, as it is now known, built in 1756–9, followed the principle of the shape of the oak tree, being broad and well rooted at its base and tapering gently towards its top, in order to withstand both the constant buffeting of the sea as well as the howling of the gales. Added stability was achieved by dovetailing the foundation blocks and pegging the stones with oak bolts. Smeaton's Tower was a triumph of engineering, which defied the gloom and doom of its critics' predictions that a stone tower would surely be swept away before long. In fact, it fulfilled its purpose from 1759 to 1882, and was only replaced because the rock on which it stood had been eroded by the pounding of the sea. Such was the esteem and affection in which it was held that Smeaton's Tower, or at any rate its upper section, was removed block by block and brought to Plymouth, where it was re-erected on The Hoe and ceremonially re-opened in 1884. It is a moving experience to visit the cramped quarters of the lighthouse keepers today, and to note that only two bunk beds were provided for the three men stationed there, since one of them would of course always be on duty.

Such is the savage nature of the coast of the West Country that shipwrecks over the centuries have remained endemic, in spite of the great improvements in lighthouse design. Some parts of the coast have a worse reputation than others, the north coast of Devon and Cornwall being particularly fearsome, as is recalled in the chilling couplet:

> From Padstow Point to Lundy Light
> Is a watery grave, by day or night.

The churchyards of the West Country contain countless burials from shipwrecks through the ages, such as that at St Keverne in south Cornwall which has a mass grave for the victims of the 486-ton emigrant ship *John* which in 1855 struck The Manacles, a terrifying reef about one mile off-shore. Of the 247 passengers and crew 156 were lost; and the bodies continued to be washed up onshore for several days. Obviously, such wrecks also provided a rich bounty in material goods which could be salvaged by 'the country', as the local people were collectively called. Another couplet neatly sums up the dependence of the commonfolk on the harvest of the occasional ocean storm:

> The *Eliza* of Liverpool came ashore
> To feed the hungry and clothe the poor.

Some of the poor were very poor indeed,

Sutton Harbour in Plymouth shelters a small fishing fleet, but its main occupants are nowadays leisurecraft such as yachts and cruisers.

The grave of the captain of the Caledonia, *wrecked off north Cornwall, is marked by the ship's figurehead* (right) *in the graveyard at Morwenstow.*

which explains why gangs of wreckers would follow a craft in distress for hours along the clifftops waiting to pounce on what was sometimes a paltry reward, often risking life and limb in the process. Just how the misfortune of some could mean the good fortune of others may be gauged from the perhaps apocryphal version of a Cornish child's prayer: 'God bless Vaather 'n' Mawther, 'n' zend a ship t'shore vore mornin'', and the prayer of Parson Troutbeck belongs in the same category: 'Dear God, we pray not that wrecks should happen, but that if it be Thy will they do, we pray Thee let them be to the benefit of Thy poor people of Scilly.' Then there is the tale of the Cornish parson whose sermon was interrupted by news of a wreck; he requested his flock to remain seated until he could divest himself of his cassock, 'so that we can all start fair'.

Whatever the authenticity of such stories, it must be remembered that the wreckers were really plunderers rather than people who used false lights to lure ships onto the rocks. Violence to the survivors was, however, not at all uncommon in earlier times. There was the notorious case of the shipwreck of the English fleet in 1707 on Scilly, when the Admiral Sir Cloudesley Shovell managed to struggle ashore only to be killed on the beach for the sake of an emerald ring. An ancient Act of Parliament may have been partly responsible for such crimes, since it was laid down that no ship could be considered a wreck unless all aboard were dead. Even so, there can be no excusing the atrocities committed against the exhausted survivors of shipwrecks.

The wreckers of Cornwall had a particularly bad reputation, as may be gauged by the report of John Robeson in the *English Chronicle* in 1825 who described them as 'human vultures who wait their evening prey, and often deprive of life the supplicating wretches whom the fury of the ocean has spared'. Most Cornish folk would have considered themselves grossly libelled by Robeson's remarks, and it is difficult at this remove in time to assess the truth of the matter. It is generally held that the violent deeds belonged to a more distant past; the annals of the nineteenth and twentieth centuries are filled with countless acts of heroism in saving lives which more than made up for the crimes of bygone days perpetrated by such as the notorious 'Cruel Coppinger', as described by the poet-priest Hawker of Morwenstow.

Parson Hawker was a man deeply disturbed by the ghastly toll exacted by the sea in his remote parish of Morwenstow in the northernmost corner of Cornwall. This stretch of the coast is extremely perilous, and there is a reminder of that fact in the graveyard of the church where the figurehead of the 500-ton *Caledonia* marks the spot where her captain lies buried. Some forty other mariners are laid to rest by the 'Upper Trees'. Hawker's ministry at Morwenstow, a place imbued with the long traditions of smuggling and wrecking, was described by the eccentric parson himself as 'the effort to do good against their will to our fellow men.' One of his more unpleasant duties was to give a Christian burial to the drowned victims of shipwreck who washed up on the shores of his parish with sickening regularity. He paid a generous reward to his parishioners for bringing the bodies to him; and when the corpses were too awful through decomposition, he would distribute doses of gin to those concerned with the burial. Hawker's vibrant and eccentric personality can still be savoured in his poems and other writings. The rectory he built, whose chimneys feature the towers of churches in which he served, is now a private residence, but Hawker's Hut, a snug shelter made from driftwood on the clifftop, is in the care of the National Trust. According to the NT notes it was here that Hawker 'clad in seaman's jersey and seaboots with his cassock, smoked pipes of opium, meditated and wrote his poetry'. One can still make the same short trek from the churchyard at Morwenstow across the fields and along the cliff and sit on the

Parson Hawker's hut on the cliffs at Morwenstow is made of driftwood from wrecks.

wooden bench where Parson Hawker spent so many hours and enjoy the same exhilarating view from this sheltered eyrie out over the open sea.

Smuggling, by the very clandestine nature of the activity, has left no trace behind it, but in the eighteenth century almost every cove and inlet had some association with contraband, which was generally regarded by the entire population as a legitimate undertaking. The Preventive men were sometimes in league with the smugglers, and more often intimidated by them. It was only gradually that the endemic smuggling of the region was brought under control by a professional body of coastguards and customs officers. At the same time, a more positive attitude towards the saving of life at sea became widespread. 1824 saw the beginning of what was to become the Royal National Lifeboat Institution, which has performed so many acts of selfless heroism. One of the most amazing exploits was the saga of

The old waterfront at Weymouth is now used by leisure craft.

Bayard's Cove at Dartmouth (right) *is redolent of the eighteenth century but is still home to H. M. Customs & Excise.*

H.M. CUSTOMS
AND EXCISE

The statue of George III at Weymouth commemorates royal patronage of Melcombe Regis.

the Lynmouth lifeboat, the *Louisa*, which was called out on 12 January 1899 to assist a vessel in distress off Porlock Weir. Unable to launch the boat at Lynmouth due to heavy seas, it was decided to haul the boat overland the twelve miles to Porlock over Countisbury Hill some 1400 feet above sea level. To add to the difficulty of this Herculean task, it was discovered that the road was too narrow in places, causing the removal of walls and hedges, all being achieved in the darkness and driving rain. One old lady was awakened in the night to learn that a corner of her house was to be demolished to allow the lifeboat to pass. The *Louisa* was eventually launched around 5.30 in the morning and went directly to the assistance of the vessel *Forest Hall*. The lifeboat crew ended up that evening in Wales, having toiled nonstop for twenty-four hours without any nourishment or respite, but succeeded in escorting the

Forest Hall which was brought under tow to the safety of Barry.

The most dramatic change to the ports and harbours of the West Country over the past hundred years has been the switch from traditional fishing and commercial activities in most cases to a new role as seaside resorts. In several places the process began in the eighteenth century. It was the health-giving attributes of sea-bathing, and for a while of actually taking the waters, which drew visitors to places such as Lyme Regis, visited by Jane Austen in 1804. The novelist indulged liberally in bathing in the chilly waters of the sea, and then had Musgrove in *Persuasion* do likewise. Melcombe was selected by George III in 1789 for a period of convalescence, and his royal patronage launched the seaside town on a glorious new career as a resort bearing the name of Melcombe Regis. In PR terms this was quite a turn for the better, since Melcombe's previous claim to fame was as the place where the black rat came ashore in 1348 carrying the fleas which caused the outbreak of the Black Death. The aristocratic tone of the new, and health-giving Melcombe Regis is set by the architecture of the Esplanade. At the south end of this noble seafront thoroughfare stands a statue of George III, erected in 1809 by 'The grateful inhabitants', and to this day they are still grateful enough to keep George III brightly painted like a medieval patron saint and to protect the statue of their benefactor by a stout iron fence.

Ilfracombe rose to be the leading resort in north Devon during the nineteenth century.

54

Seaside towns often indulge in bold colour schemes, and nowhere can this be seen to more dramatic effect than in Appledore's Irsha Street (left)*. A more tasteful, Classical appearance is provided by Torquay's Montpelier* (above)*.*

The drydock at Bristol where Brunel's iron steamship, SS Great Britain, *was originally built.*

Melcombe was in fact merged with Weymouth as early as 1571, but the name has lingered on.

During the Napoleonic wars when travel to the Continent was virtually impossible, seaside tourism in the West Country really took off. Sidmouth was patronised by the Duke and Duchess of Kent and the Marquess of Bute *inter alia*, and has maintained a vestige of its exclusive allure. Teignmouth was another select watering place. Torquay was first patronised by the Navy, which established a base there for warding off attacks by the French, but within a few years some of the houses built for naval officers and their families were being let to visitors, and the 'Queen of watering places' was poised for a dramatic development. Penzance was described as early as 1795 as 'the Montpellier of England'. Lynmouth was visited by Percy and Mary Shelley in 1812; and Coleridge was introduced by the Wordsworths to the area behind Porlock, which, like the Lake District, had all the rugged, romantic grandeur of an 'English Switzerland'.

Ilfracombe also received a boost during the Napoleonic wars and went on to make tourism its prime industry, attracting in its heyday before the Great War several members of European royal families including the future Kaiser Wilhelm. Like many other ports Ilfracombe made up for its declining fisheries by seasonal visitors, and the resident population catering for them rose almost fivefold in the course of the nineteenth century. The bracing air of the north Devon coast was greatly praised, but Ilfracombe's bathing facilities were limited until a tunnel was driven through the cliffs to give access to more of the coast. Two bathing pools – a strict segregation of ladies and gentlemen was enforced – were filled twice daily by the incoming tide. The tunnelling was carried out allegedly by miners from south Wales; and indeed the cavortings of Welsh daytrippers who arrived by steamer and earned themselves the nickname of the 'merry Cymri' caused some embarrassment to the more respectable citizens of Ilfracombe.

Many seaside resorts were transformed by the coming of the Great Western Railway. By 1861 Torquay's population had reached 11,000 compared to only 1,000 in 1801. Newquay and St Ives switched wholeheartedly from pilchards to tourists, both species preferring the same sandy bays. Of the former place Murray's *Handbook for Cornwall* noted in 1893: 'the terminus of the Great Western Railway has made a small and inaccessible fishing village into a rising watering place.' Where the railway did not penetrate, such as Salcombe, tourism had to await the era of the motor coach and private car, which are now the mainstay of so many coastal towns.

It was during the middle years of the twentieth century that tourism became almost synonymous with the West Country, obscuring the many activities which had previously sustained the region. Heavy shipbuilding was one such industry, and there is no more potent relic of that proud heritage than the *SS Great Britain*, launched in Bristol in 1843 as the first screw-driven iron ship to cross the Atlantic. The revolutionary design by Brunel regained for Britain the initiative in the Atlantic trade which had been lost to America. After a prestigious international career as an ocean liner the *SS Great Britain* ended up as a floating store in the Falklands, and in 1937 she was ignominiously beached in Sparrow Cove. In 1970 the *SS Great Britain* was salvaged and brought back to the very dock in Bristol where her iron keel had been laid almost a hundred years previously. Although now reduced to a long retirement as a museum piece in a drydock the *SS Great Britain* is a telling reminder of heroic achievements, and stands as a reminder of the maritime heritage of the West Country as a whole.

(Overleaf) *St Ives, now home to tourists instead of pilchards.*

SS93

A Renaissance-style memorial in Sherborne Abbey for John Leweston and his wife.

Select Bibliography

Alcock, Leslie, *Arthur's Britain*, Penguin 1973
Ashe, Geoffrey, *The Landscape of King Arthur*, Webb & Bower 1987
Atkinson, R. J. C., *Stonehenge*, Penguin 1979
Balchin, W. G. V., *The Cornish Landscape*, Hodder & Stoughton 1983
Barton, D. B., *A History of Tin Mining and Smelting in Cornwall*, Barton 1967
— *A History of Copper Mining in Devon and Cornwall*, Barton 1968
— *The Cornish Beam Engine*, Barton 1966
Burton S. H., *The West Country*, Robert Hale 1972
Berry, Claude, *Portrait of Cornwall*, Robert Hale 1984
Bettey, J. H., *Wessex from AD 1000*, Longman 1986
Bidwell, Paul T., *Roman Exeter: Fortress and Town*, Exeter Museum Service 1980
Booker, Frank, *The Industrial Archaeology of the Tamar Valley*, David & Charles 1971
— *The Great Western Railway*, David St John Thomas 1985
Burl, Aubrey, *Prehistoric Avebury*, Yale University Press 1979
Chippindale, Christopher, *Stonehenge Complete*, Thames & Hudson 1983
Coles, Bryony & John, *Sweet Track to Glastonbury*, Thames & Hudson 1986
Cunliffe, Barry, *Roman Bath Discovered*, Routledge and Kegan Paul 1984
— *The City of Bath*, Sutton 1986
Doble, G. H., *The Saints of Cornwall* (series), Dean & Chapter, Truro
du Maurier, Daphne, *Vanishing Cornwall*, Penguin 1972
Dyer, James, *Southern England: An Archaeological Guide*, Faber 1977
Fox, Lady Aileen, *South West England*, David & Charles 1973
Hadfield, E. C. R., *The Canals of South West England*, David & Charles 1967
Harris, Helen, *The Industrial Archaeology of Dartmoor*, David & Charles 1986
Hudson, Kenneth, *The Industrial Archaeology of Southern England*, David & Charles 1968
Jenner/Gomme/Little, *Bristol, An Architectural History*, Lund Humphries 1979
John, Catherine Rachel, *The Saints of Cornwall*, Lodenek 1981
Kay-Robinson, Denys, *Devon and Cornwall*, Bartholomew 1977
— *The Landscape of Thomas Hardy*, Webb & Bower 1984
Parker, Derek, *The West Country and the Sea*, Longman 1980
Pearce, Susan M., *The Kingdom of Dumnonia*, Lodenek 1978
— *The Archaeology of SW Britain*, Collins 1981
Pettit, Paul, *Devon, Cornwall and the Isles of Scilly*, Michael Joseph 1987
Pevsner, Sir Nikolaus, *Buildings of England* (series) Penguin
— *Cornwall*
— *Dorset*
— *Devon*
— *North Somerset and Bristol*
— *South and West Somerset*
— *Wiltshire*
Ponting, K. G., *The Woollen Industry of South West England*, Adams & Dart 1971
Sale, Richard, *Dorset*, Hutchinson 1985
Taylor, Christopher, *Dorset (The Making of the English Landscape)*, Hodder & Stoughton 1970
Thomas, Charles, *Exploration of a Drowned Landscape: Archaeology and History of the Isles of Scilly*, Batsford 1985
Todd, Malcolm, *The South West to AD 100*, Longman 1987

Hardy's Cottage, Higher Bockhampton, Dorset.

Index

Note: Cor=Cornwall; Dev=Devon; Dor=Dorset; Wilts=Wiltshire. Page numbers in *italics* refer to illustrations.